The Tea Party Movement

Other Books in the Current Controversies Series

Drug Legalization
Factory Farming
Forensic Technology
The Green Movement
Medical Ethics
Nuclear Energy
Oil
Teen Pregnancy and Parenting
Vegetarianism

The Tea Party Movement

Debra A. Miller, Book Editor

GREENHAVEN PRESS
A part of Gale, Cengage Learning

Detroit • New York • San Francisco • New Haven, Conn • Waterville, Maine • London

Elizabeth Des Chenes, *Managing Editor*

© 2012 Greenhaven Press, a part of Gale, Cengage Learning

Gale and Greenhaven Press are registered trademarks used herein under license.

For more information, contact:
Greenhaven Press
27500 Drake Rd.
Farmington Hills, MI 48331-3535
Or you can visit our Internet site at gale.cengage.com

ALL RIGHTS RESERVED.
No part of this work covered by the copyright herein may be reproduced, transmitted, stored, or used in any form or by any means graphic, electronic, or mechanical, including but not limited to photocopying, recording, scanning, digitizing, taping, Web distribution, information networks, or information storage and retrieval systems, except as permitted under Section 107 or 108 of the 1976 United States Copyright Act, without the prior written permission of the publisher.

For product information and technology assistance, contact us at

Gale Customer Support, 1-800-877-4253
For permission to use material from this text or product, submit all requests online at www.cengage.com/permissions

Further permissions questions can be emailed to permissionrequest@cengage.com

Articles in Greenhaven Press anthologies are often edited for length to meet page requirements. In addition, original titles of these works are changed to clearly present the main thesis and to explicitly indicate the author's opinion. Every effort is made to ensure that Greenhaven Press accurately reflects the original intent of the authors. Every effort has been made to trace the owners of copyrighted material.

Cover image © David Howells/Corbis.

LIBRARY OF CONGRESS CATALOGING-IN-PUBLICATION DATA

The Tea Party Movement / Debra A. Miller, book editor.
   p. cm. -- (Current controversies)
   Includes bibliographical references and index.
   ISBN 978-0-7377-5636-4 (hardcover) -- ISBN 978-0-7377-5637-1 (pbk.)
   1. Tea Party movement. 2. United States--Politics and government--2009- I. Miller, Debra A.
   JK2391.T43T43 2011
   320.520973--dc22
                                                              2011011695

Printed in the USA
  2 3 4 5 6   30 29 28 27 26

Contents

Foreword 15

Introduction 18

Chapter 1: Is the Tea Party a Legitimate Political Movement?

Chapter Preface 23

Yes: The Tea Party Is a Legitimate Political Movement

The Tea Party Is a Grassroots Organization Representing Mainstream Concerns 26
J. Wesley Fox

The Tea Party movement is a unique, grassroots collection of citizens' groups that are worried about the direction the country is headed and concerned about issues such as excessive government spending, the economy, and the expansion of government power. The Tea Party's supporters are largely mainstream Americans who are frustrated with both Democrats and Republicans and who are interested in using legitimate political activity to change Washington.

The Tea Party Had Many Key Victories in the 2010 Midterm Elections 31
Mary Claire Kendall

Tea Party activists are angry at a government that they view as too big and too aligned with wealthy corporations that do not care about ordinary, hardworking Americans. The Tea Party used that anger in the 2010 midterm elections to retake the House of Representatives for Republicans, in addition to several Senate seats.

The Tea Party Has a Good Chance at Remaining Viable 34
Justin Quinn

Only time will tell whether the Tea Party movement can be sustained long term, but it has several advantages. For example, the Tea Party has attracted experienced political operatives and has acquired the financial backing of big business. These factors give the Tea Party a good foundation for future growth.

No: The Tea Party Is Not a Legitimate Political Movement

The Tea Party Is Not a Genuine Political Movement   38
Stuart Whatley

America is known for its history of successful social and political movements, but the Tea Party is not a legitimate movement in this tradition. Rather, the Tea Party has no clear goals, coherent messages, or solutions to the country's problems, and it is an example of the exploitation of frustrated Americans by corporate interests.

The Tea Party's Importance Has Been Exaggerated   43
Stephanie Mencimer

The Tea Party's power has been exaggerated, because it lacks the essential capacity to oppose big corporate interests. This was seen in Congress's 2010 passage of a food safety bill that was supported by large agricultural interests and in the earlier passage of a health care bill that was backed by the insurance industry. Even the angriest group of grassroots activists are no match for corporate money.

The Tea Party Is a Movement Funded and Exploited by Corporations   47
Larisa Alexandrovna

The United States does need a third party but not the Tea Party, whose members lack a basic understanding of American history. The Boston Tea Party was a protest against corporate interests, yet the Tea Party movement is actually funded by corporations and is used as a pawn to achieve corporate interests.

Most American Voters Oppose the Tea Party as a Third Party   50
Sean J. Miller

The rise of the Tea Party movement shows that the American public is unhappy with both Democrats and Republicans, but most voters do not want the Tea Party to be the alternative third party. A 2010 poll found that 54 percent of respondents favored a third party but two-thirds of Democrats, 42 percent of independents, and 45 percent of Republicans rejected the Tea Party as the third party choice.

Chapter 2: Is the Tea Party Movement Racist?

Chapter Preface 55

Yes: The Tea Party Movement Is Racist

Tea Party Activists Include White Nationalists and Other Racists 57
Bill Berkowitz

One of the issues that could derail the Tea Party is the charge of racism. This charge has arisen because Tea Party activists tend to be almost all white and because some supporters have shown up at rallies with racist signs and slogans. This racist element must be eliminated for the Tea Party to become an effective political force.

Tea Party Supporters Are Upset About a Black President 62
Eugene Robinson

It is not racist to criticize President Barack Obama, but the Tea Party's vitriolic attacks on the president are difficult to explain without considering the possibility of racial prejudice. Tea Party supporters claim they want to take their country back, but no such rhetoric was heard during the presidency of George W. Bush, despite his legacy of two wars, large deficit spending, and creation of the Troubled Asset Relief Program (TARP). The only factor that makes Obama different is his race.

The Tea Party Is All About Race 66
Bob Cesca

The explanations of Tea Party members for why they are so outraged by President Barack Obama are nonsensical, so the real reason for their anger is likely race. In reality, the Tea Party is just an extension of conservative talk radio and the Fox News network, which is known for race-baiting and outright racism.

No: The Tea Party Movement Is Not Racist

The Tea Party Is Not a Haven for Racists 72
Cathy Young

A University of Washington poll on racist attitudes among supporters of the Tea Party found that Tea Partiers are similar to mainstream Americans in this regard. Although it is true that Tea Party supporters are mostly white, more likely to be male, and staunchly Republican and conservative, this does not make them racists.

Race Is Not the Motivator Behind Tea Party Activism 77
Robert Chapman-Smith

The claims that the Tea Party is motivated by race are unfounded because the movement's anger did not begin with and is not directed solely at President Barack Obama. The roots of the Tea Party's rage are a repudiation of George W. Bush's presidency; to ignore this history is intellectually lazy.

African American Tea Party Activists See No Racism in the Movement 80
Aaron Goldstein

Liberal commentators are using allegations of racism as a weapon to discredit the Tea Party. However, black Tea Party supporters say that these charges are completely fabricated. It is really the Tea Party's message of small government that critics do not like.

Claims of Racism in the Tea Party Are Hyperbole 84
Michael C. Moynihan

Various commentators have compared Tea Party protests to incidents of genocide and violent racism, but there is no evidence to support claims of violence or overt racism by Tea Party activists. Instead, claims of Tea Party racism are just examples of heated rhetoric that should be toned down.

Chapter 3: Is the Tea Party Movement Compatible with the Republican Party?

Chapter Preface 91

Yes: The Tea Party Movement Is Compatible with the Republican Party

Tea Party Activists Are Just Republicans by Another Name 94

Perrspectives

The 2010 midterm elections will likely mark the end of the Tea Party movement because Tea Party activists are really just Republicans. They vote Republican; they tend to be white, male, and higher-income; and their policy goals are Republican—e.g., opposing health care reform and cap-and-trade energy legislation, and supporting tax cuts for the wealthy. Now that Republicans are winning again, there will be no need for Tea Party activism.

The Tea Party Is Just More Republican Radicalism 99

Tim Rutten

In the 2010 midterm elections, Tea Party and Republican candidates criticized President Barack Obama as radical and accused him of leading the country into socialism. In reality, the Republican Party has nominated some of the most radical candidates America has seen in more than a century, and there is little difference between the views of the Tea Party and more mainstream Republicans.

The Tea Party Message Is an Ultraconservative Republican One 103

Ole Ole Olson

The Tea Party is a fledgling grassroots movement that was taken over by corporate groups in response to the progressive awakening that was threatening to change policies in ways that corporations did not support. These corporate players then changed the Tea Party message from a libertarian one to an ultraconservative, Republican one. The Tea Party's new policy statement—the Contract from America—reveals this message clearly.

No: The Tea Party Movement Is Not Compatible with the Republican Party

Tea Party Libertarians Are Fundamentally at Odds with Republicans 112
Glenn Greenwald

The Republican Party is trying to reinvent itself by absorbing the energy of the libertarian Tea Party movement, but this will not work because Republicans and libertarians are completely incompatible. Republican rule is always characterized by expanded government powers and deficit spending, but when they are out of power Republicans like to pretend they are for small government. This fraud will soon be exposed.

The Tea Party Disagrees with Republican Positions on Foreign Policy 117
Barry Gewen

Although it is difficult to clarify the Tea Party's positions on foreign policy issues, it is likely that Tea Party supporters will challenge many mainstream Republican ideas. For example, the Tea Party is suspicious of free trade, which the Republican Party has always supported, and of other foreign policy issues such as American troops in Afghanistan and Iraq; the Tea Party may find more in common with Democrats.

The Tea Party Will Cause Republicans to Lose the 2012 Presidential Election 123
Mark Shields

Historically, grassroots insurgent groups such as the Tea Party terrify party leaders, prompting them to adopt the insurgent group's positions. This happened to the Democratic Party when antiwar protestors during the Vietnam War caused the party to become antiwar, and it is likely that the Republican Party will pander to the Tea Party in the same way. This could help President Barack Obama win reelection in 2012.

Chapter 4: What Is the Future of the Tea Party Movement?

Chapter Preface 127

The 2010 Midterm Elections Begin a Period   130
of Increased Tea Party Activism
  *Jennifer Levitz, Cameron McWhirter, and Douglas
  A. Blackmon*
  Although some Tea Party candidates lost in the 2010 midterm elections, the many Tea Party wins suggest that the movement could become a major force in Congress. Supporters say that the elections are just the beginning of their fight for smaller government, with some Tea Party groups organizing around issues such as balancing the federal budget and repealing health care reform.

The Tea Party Will Be Betrayed by   134
Corporate-Funded Politicians
  Dave Johnson
  Tea Party supporters oppose free trade agreements, bank bailouts, and other policies favored by corporate America, but many Tea Party candidates were funded by these same corporations. It is likely, therefore, that Tea Party members of Congress will vote against the interests of the Tea Party on issues important to their funding sources.

The Tea Party Will Survive Only as   138
a Republican Party Faction
  Matt Steinglass
  The Tea Party movement has some progressive commentators worried about its extremist views, but often right-wing parties tend to flame out quickly. The Tea Party, however, might have a more lasting impact largely because it has been organized as a faction within the Republican Party. This might allow the movement another couple of years of protests.

The Tea Party Will Soon Be Absorbed   141
by the Republican Party
  Doyle McManus
  Once a grassroots organization angry with both political parties, the Tea Party is rapidly becoming a part of the Republican Party, helping it to rebrand itself as a party concerned with fiscal issues. There is no question, however, that the Republican Party will soon co-opt and absorb the Tea Party, causing its demise.

The Tea Party Must Take Over the   145
Republican Party to Succeed
  James R. Keena
    After winning in the 2010 midterm elections, the Tea Party must define a path forward for the country based on limited government principles. The best way to do this is to engulf and take control of the Republican Party. The Tea Party then must try to create a big-tent program that will attract a broad spectrum of the electorate—one that embraces not only limited government but also principles such as fiscal responsibility, economic growth, and a strong national defense.

The Tea Party Will Fail if It Embraces   156
Conservative Social Issues
  Jim Yardley
    After the Tea Party's wins in the 2010 midterm elections, some conservatives have called for the Tea Party to embrace conservative social issues such as abortion and same-sex marriage. This would be a mistake, however, because social issues are not important to voters at this time. Including these issues in the Tea Party's agenda would only keep the Democrats in power.

Tea Party Ideologues May   160
Prevent Constructive Lawmaking
by Reasonable Republicans
  Steve Benen
    Reasonable congressional Republicans have been put on notice by the Tea Party that they may be targeted for defeat in the 2012 election cycle if they do not embrace extremist Tea Party policies. This threat may hinder Congress from constructive policy making and push even moderate Republicans to adopt obstructionist stances.

The Tea Party Could Produce   163
Political Chaos
  Steven J. Gulitti

The Tea Party will soon find that governing is much harder than winning elections. The Tea Party's rhetoric must now be reconciled with political realities such as Congress's institutional nature, the difficulty of achieving spending cuts during an economic slowdown, and the power of lobbyists and wealthy special interests. Instead of an acceptance of Tea Party values, the result could be political chaos.

Organizations to Contact   172

Bibliography   175

Index   180

Foreword

By definition, controversies are "discussions of questions in which opposing opinions clash" (Webster's Twentieth Century Dictionary Unabridged). Few would deny that controversies are a pervasive part of the human condition and exist on virtually every level of human enterprise. Controversies transpire between individuals and among groups, within nations and between nations. Controversies supply the grist necessary for progress by providing challenges and challengers to the status quo. They also create atmospheres where strife and warfare can flourish. A world without controversies would be a peaceful world; but it also would be, by and large, static and prosaic.

The Series' Purpose

The purpose of the Current Controversies series is to explore many of the social, political, and economic controversies dominating the national and international scenes today. Titles selected for inclusion in the series are highly focused and specific. For example, from the larger category of criminal justice, Current Controversies deals with specific topics such as police brutality, gun control, white collar crime, and others. The debates in Current Controversies also are presented in a useful, timeless fashion. Articles and book excerpts included in each title are selected if they contribute valuable, long-range ideas to the overall debate. And wherever possible, current information is enhanced with historical documents and other relevant materials. Thus, while individual titles are current in focus, every effort is made to ensure that they will not become quickly outdated. Books in the Current Controversies series will remain important resources for librarians, teachers, and students for many years.

In addition to keeping the titles focused and specific, great care is taken in the editorial format of each book in the series. Book introductions and chapter prefaces are offered to provide background material for readers. Chapters are organized around several key questions that are answered with diverse opinions representing all points on the political spectrum. Materials in each chapter include opinions in which authors clearly disagree as well as alternative opinions in which authors may agree on a broader issue but disagree on the possible solutions. In this way, the content of each volume in Current Controversies mirrors the mosaic of opinions encountered in society. Readers will quickly realize that there are many viable answers to these complex issues. By questioning each author's conclusions, students and casual readers can begin to develop the critical thinking skills so important to evaluating opinionated material.

Current Controversies is also ideal for controlled research. Each anthology in the series is composed of primary sources taken from a wide gamut of informational categories including periodicals, newspapers, books, US and foreign government documents, and the publications of private and public organizations. Readers will find factual support for reports, debates, and research papers covering all areas of important issues. In addition, an annotated table of contents, an index, a book and periodical bibliography, and a list of organizations to contact are included in each book to expedite further research.

Perhaps more than ever before in history, people are confronted with diverse and contradictory information. During the Persian Gulf War, for example, the public was not only treated to minute-to-minute coverage of the war, it was also inundated with critiques of the coverage and countless analyses of the factors motivating US involvement. Being able to sort through the plethora of opinions accompanying today's major issues, and to draw one's own conclusions, can be a complicated and frustrating struggle. It is the editors' hope that Current Controversies will help readers with this struggle.

Introduction

> *"Today's Tea Party movement ... is a protest against the US government, based mostly on fears that the federal government has grown too powerful and too fiscally irresponsible."*

The Tea Party movement, a loosely organized coalition of grassroots citizens' political groups, is named after the 1773 Boston Tea Party. The original Boston Tea Party was a political protest by early American colonists against Britain over that country's imposition of taxes on American settlers without giving them representation in the British Parliament. Today's Tea Party movement, however, is a protest against the US government, based mostly on fears that the federal government has grown too powerful and is fiscally irresponsible.

Many commentators say the modern Tea Party movement can be traced to Ron Paul, a libertarian Republican congressman from Texas who ran in 2008 as a candidate for the Republican nomination for the US presidency. As a libertarian, Paul opposed government involvement in the lives of Americans on many levels. He spoke out against deficit spending, taxes, business regulation, government security intrusions such as wiretapping, and the wars in Iraq and Afghanistan. Paul's views were not popular in the Republican Party, so on December 16, 2007, Paul and his supporters marched from Boston City Hall to the historic Faneuil Hall, where they held a fund-raising rally that appealed for grassroots support, raising $4.3 million in one day over the Internet. Ron Paul's bid for the presidency ultimately failed, but many of his libertarian ideas ultimately became part of Tea Party philosophy. Like Ron Paul, today's Tea Party protesters generally complain that the federal government has grown too big, that it taxes citizens too much, and that it has taken on too much debt. Although their goals are not completely defined, most Tea Party activists want to see smaller government, lower taxes, reduced federal debt, and a balanced federal budget.

Following a Republican defeat and the election of the Democratic presidential candidate Barack Obama in the fall of 2008, many of Ron Paul's supporters and other conservative Republicans became even more energized. By then, the economic recession was in full swing, and the federal government's response was a $700 billion Troubled Asset Relief Program (TARP)—a program initiated by President George W. Bush and continued by President Obama. Although economists viewed TARP as critical to preventing another Great Depression, many people saw it as an unjustified bailout of Wall Street at taxpayers' expense. Other policies proposed by President Obama, such as an economic stimulus program and health care reform, also were viewed by many conservative citizens as unnecessary deficit spending and examples of a bloated and out-of-control federal government. These concerns became the foundation of a fledgling Tea Party movement.

The seed of a national, organized Tea Party protest, however, is deemed to have been planted on February 19, 2009, when CNBC reporter Rick Santelli engaged in a now-famous rant on the floor of the Chicago Mercantile Exchange against government bank bailouts and help for struggling homeowners, who he called losers. Santelli called for a new American Tea Party to protest these policies. Santelli's rant was captured on video and soon spread widely over the Internet, leading to the organizing of Tea Party rallies and summits around the country throughout the remainder of 2009.

The Tea Party also began endorsing candidates to run in the Republican primaries in preparation for the 2010 midterm congressional and state elections. A number of Tea Party candidates won in the primaries, ousting long-term, mainstream

Republican incumbents. Along the way, the Tea Party attracted widespread media attention as well as vocal support from some Republicans. Former Alaskan governor and vice presidential candidate Sarah Palin, for example, openly aligned herself with the Tea Party. A number of prominent Tea Party candidates were elected into office in the 2010 midterms, most notably the son of Ron Paul, Rand Paul, who was elected to the US Senate by Kentucky voters.

Critics have pointed out, however, that many of the so-called grassroots Tea Party events and candidates received funding from corporate sponsors. One of the main sources of funding identified by numerous reporters, for example, was a group called Americans for Prosperity, a libertarian organization started and funded by billionaire businessman David H. Koch that helped to train and educate Tea Party protesters about policy and effective political organizing. Koch and his brother Charles run Koch Industries, a huge corporate conglomerate estimated to be the second-largest company in America. Only billionaires Bill Gates and Warren Buffett are richer than the Koch brothers. The Koch brothers are also well-known conservatives who have opposed President Obama's policies and have spent large sums of money fighting climate change legislation, perhaps because Koch Industries is one of the country's biggest environmental polluters. Because of this corporate backing, many critics complain that the Tea Party is not a true grassroots organization but rather a bunch of naive citizens who are being manipulated by corporate interests. Other criticisms of the Tea Party have included claims that its supporters are mainly older, white, relatively wealthy Republicans who hold racist views—ideas stoked by the virtual absence of people of color in the organization and the appearance of some questionably racist signs at some Tea Party rallies.

Many progressives see the Tea Party as both extremist and hypocritical in its views—the latter critique arises from statements of some supporters who decry government spending yet do not want to lose their own Social Security or Medicare benefits. Conservatives, on the other hand, have largely embraced the Tea Party, although some have questioned whether the Tea Party will truly change the Republican Party position on issues, making it more right-wing in its views, or whether the Tea Party will simply become a vocal but ineffective faction within the Republican Party.

The viewpoints in *Current Controversies: The Tea Party Movement* address many of the issues that have arisen concerning this recent political movement. Authors in this volume debate whether the Tea Party movement is legitimate, whether it is racist, whether it is compatible with the Republican Party, and whether it will survive or have any political impact on the nation's future.

CHAPTER 1

Is the Tea Party a Legitimate Political Movement?

Chapter Preface

Tea Party protests proliferated during 2009, and the Tea Party supported dozens of candidates in the fall 2010 midterm elections for the US Senate and House of Representatives. Many of the Tea Party–backed candidates in the general elections were victors over establishment Republicans in earlier primary races. In the end, the Tea Party won a number of important 2010 races, electing enough ultraconservative Republicans to allow the Republican Party to wrest back majority control of the House from Democrats. This result helped to solidify the power of the grassroots protest movement within the Republican Party, and it may have been a harbinger of future Tea Party political influence.

In fact, the Tea Party demonstrated its electoral power even before the midterm elections, in a special election held in early 2010. The occasion was a race in Massachusetts to fill the US Senate seat of former Democratic senator Edward "Ted" Kennedy, following his death in August 2009. After winning the Republican primary in a landslide, Massachusetts state legislator Scott Brown won in the special general election in January 2010, easily defeating the Democratic nominee, Massachusetts attorney general Martha Coakley. Although Scott Brown did not identify himself as a Tea Party candidate, Tea Party groups endorsed his campaign and paid for television ads supporting his campaign. Brown's victory marked the first time a Republican had won the Massachusetts Senate seat since 1953, and many commentators claimed it as a Tea Party win.

It was in the 2010 midterms, however, that the Tea Party really flexed its political muscles. Nearly 140 candidates in the US congressional midterm elections were supported by the Tea Party, and some estimates said that thirty of these candidates ultimately won, defeating Democratic opponents. Some political experts called this a Tea Party tidal wave, while others maintained that the results were mixed. Either way, what is certain is that Tea Party–backed candidates won in several key races. One of the most prominent of these was Rand Paul, son of Ron Paul and a self-identified Tea Party activist, who was elected to the US Senate as a Republican from Kentucky. Another important race took place in Florida; Tea Party candidate Marco Rubio won the US Senate seat, beating not only the Democratic candidate but also former moderate Republican Florida governor Charlie Crist, who ran as an independent. In addition, high-profile Tea Party candidate Nikki Haley was elected governor of South Carolina, after receiving an endorsement from Tea Party supporter Sarah Palin.

The wins by Tea Party–backed candidates in the midterm elections helped Republicans seize a majority in the US House of Representatives. This victory was clear and unmistakable. Although Republicans only needed thirty-nine seats to win back control of the House, Republicans gained at least sixty House seats in the November 2, 2010, elections, and Tea Party–endorsed candidates accounted for twenty-eight of those wins. Republicans also won seats in the Senate, but not enough to oust Democratic control. Two very flamboyant Tea Party candidates lost their bid for the Senate, allowing the Democrats to hold seats in Delaware and Nevada. In Delaware, observers say Christine O'Donnell never established herself as a credible candidate after video footage of several odd past statements were publicized. Another candidate, Sharron Angle, failed to unseat Senate Majority Leader Harry Reid, after Reid portrayed her as a political extremist who advocated eliminating Social Security and using gun remedies to address political problems.

The big questions after the 2010 elections were whether the Tea Party would be able to maintain its influence and whether it can have an impact on legislation. The realities of governing, after all, are much different from campaign challenges. Newly elected Tea Party legislators on Capitol Hill will be vastly outnumbered by establishment Republicans and Democrats, and legislation often results from compromise rather than an insistence on maintaining strict ideological views or positions like those asserted by many Tea Party advocates. Although many Americans might support Tea Party ideas of smaller government and debt reduction, some political experts say this support could vanish once specific proposals are advanced that affect middle-class entitlement programs such as health care, Medicare, or Social Security. Another concern is whether the Tea Party legislators will be able to stand up to their corporate sponsors, who may not be interested in achieving key Tea Party goals.

The authors of the viewpoints contained in this chapter address some of the questions involving whether the Tea Party is a legitimate political movement and whether it will remain viable in US politics.

The Tea Party Is a Grassroots Organization Representing Mainstream Concerns

J. Wesley Fox

J. Wesley Fox is chairman of Restore America's Legacy, a political action committee. He is a recent graduate of DePaul University College of Law and has been active in local and national politics for several years.

In the last few decades there has been no political movement comparable to the Tea Party. The Tea Party movement is unique because it is entirely grassroots and desires to change American politics from the bottom up. The mainstream media and the Democratic leadership all misunderstand and grossly underestimate the movement. They have labeled it a movement of extreme right-wing nuts that are angry at having a black president, or don't want to pay taxes, or "cling to guns and religion."

They are wrong. In fact, the Tea Party movement is a mainstream "awakening" that has been long overdue and will not wither and die within a couple years as some predict.

Tea Party Concerns

The Tea Party groups are a loose and decentralized coalition of libertarians, conservatives, disenchanted independents and moderate democrats. Tea Partiers are not a concentrated group of ideologues but a diverse collection of regular groups that are alarmed at the direction of the country. It began with the wasteful Stimulus Package [the American Recovery and Reinvestment Act of 2009, enacted by Congress in February 2009]

J. Wesley Fox, "Tea Party Movement Has Had a Positive Impact on American Politics," Right Side News, August 2, 2010. www.rightsidenews.com. Copyright © 2010 by J. Wesley Fox. All rights reserved. Reproduced by permission of Right Side News.

and was further amplified by taxes built into cap'n'trade[1] and health care reform. Tea Partiers are also upset at the corruption and utter lack of transparency in the [President Barack] Obama administration and the Democratic Congress.

The biggest issues for Tea Partiers are excessive government spending, the economy and the expansion of government power over the past two years. Some Tea Party groups may have additional issues of concern or have differing priorities but nearly all Tea Party groups share these concerns. Tea Partiers also share three core ideals: (1) limited government/individual freedom; (2) fiscal responsibility; and (3) free markets. They strongly support limiting the power of the federal government and are alarmed at the dramatic increase in federal power. Tea Partiers are also outraged at the massive budget deficits, the growth of the national debt, and the generational theft [stealing money from future generations through wasteful spending] taking place. Finally, they are strong proponents of economic freedom and believe strongly that President Obama and the Democratic Congress are dismantling our free market economy in favor of a more centralized, socialist economy.

Another important element of the movement is [its] attitude toward partisan politics. Tea Partiers have consistently expressed their frustration and discontent with the Republicans as well as Democrats. In general, Tea Partiers are antiestablishment and want wholesale changes in their representatives. They are highly suspicious of career politicians and the influence of the national party leadership in local elections. As a result, they have rejected the traditional or establishment candidates in a number of primaries, preferring more independent or activist candidates.

---

1. Cap and trade is an environmental policy that places a limit, or "cap," on the amount of pollutants a company is allowed to emit and requires companies to buy emissions permits.

A Mainstream Movement

The Tea Party movement is not all-white, all-conservative, violent or racist. These accusations have been thrown out without any evidence to back them up. Polls have found that supporters of the Tea Party movement are largely mainstream in terms of demographics. About 49% of Tea Party supporters are Republican while a surprising 43% are independents. They come from every socioeconomic class, age group, and ethnic group. Only 79% of Tea Party supporters are white, which is comparable to the percentage of whites in the general population. Despite the despicable accusations of Democrats and elitist media personalities, Tea Partiers are representative of the American people in almost every way.

Tea Partiers are not a concentrated group of ideologues but a diverse collection of regular groups that are alarmed at the direction of the country.

Another baseless accusation is that Tea Partiers are violent gun-touting maniacs. The movement does not advocate the violent overthrow of the government. At nearly every demonstration and protest, Tea Partiers have countless signs reading "Remember in November." Tea Partiers want change through elections not gunfire. Like any other movement, there are individuals that are unhinged and violent, but the media's focus on this extremely small sect demonstrates their lack of integrity and liberal bias. In reality, the Tea Party movement is one of the most peaceful large-scale political protests in recent memory.

An Agenda for Change Within the Republican Party

The objective of the Tea Party movement is to change the Republican Party from within. The Tea Parties have already flexed their muscle in a number of primary elections. In Illinois, the son of former Speaker [of the House of Representatives] Dennis Hastert was defeated by a lesser-known Tea Party candidate named Randy Hultgren. In the Nevada and Kentucky Senate primaries, the Republican establishment strongly supported Sue Lowden and Trey Grayson. However, their close relations with the party leadership led to suspicion and their eventual defeat to lesser-known candidates Sharron Angle and Rand Paul.

The Tea Party movement has also contributed to the removal of incumbent Republicans including Sen. Arlen Specter, who was forced to switch parties. Other defeated incumbents include Rep. Bob Inglis of South Carolina and Sen. Bob Bennett of Utah. The primaries of the past few months clearly demonstrate the Tea Party movement is very influential within the Republican Party and has already had a number of successes getting [its] own candidates on the ballot in November. In other words, [Tea Partiers] are successfully changing the party.

Polls have found that supporters of the Tea Party movement are largely mainstream in terms of demographics.

Restore America's Legacy [RAL, a conservative political action committee] and the Tea Party movement have a lot in common in terms of ideology. The Tea Party strongly supports three of RAL's five principles (limited government, fiscal responsibility, free markets). The Tea Party has also made a very strong effort to become better informed and more active in the traditional political process. RAL wishes to do the same, providing information to supporters, raising funds to support campaigns, and evaluating candidates using unique and selective criteria. Both also are highly critical of career politicians and want to support candidates with real-world experience.

The Tea Party movement is a positive development in American politics and RAL strongly supports [its] activities. If the Tea Party movement is successful in the midterm elections [November 2010] it will prove that career politicians can be held accountable and that it is the people that hold the power. It would also prove that a strong antiestablishment and antigovernment movement can manifest itself peacefully through a massive grassroots effort and legitimate political activity, not intimidation or violence. It will also strike a blow to cynics who believe that the people cannot change Washington. RAL hopes the Tea Party movement will succeed in its efforts to bring new leadership to Congress in 2010 and to the White House in 2012.

The Tea Party Had Many Key Victories in the 2010 Midterm Elections

Mary Claire Kendall

Mary Claire Kendall is an independent writer who served as special assistant to the assistant secretary for health, US Department of Health and Human Services, during the four years of President George H.W. Bush's administration.

No question, the Tea Party movement was a success in 2010, making all the difference on election night when, from Scranton [Pennsylvania] to Oshkosh [Wisconsin], the congressional district map turned from solid blue to solid red. Truly, it was a tidal wave of voter unease, expressed by a wholesale rejection of Democrats.

Tea Party Origins

The meteor that catapulted this movement was CNBC's Rick Santelli, who on February 19, 2009, called out President Barack Obama's Homeowner Affordability and Stability Plan, with its too-generous bailouts for "promoting bad behavior."

That day, Santelli raised the possibility of a "Chicago Tea Party" on April 15, 2009, to speak up for the working stiff, who was footing the bill. The idea caught on and spread like wildfire, with rallies and organizing efforts continuing well beyond that first Tax Day protest.

When Obama had the temerity to bulldoze through a health care bill that the country didn't ask for and didn't want—when jobs were the pressing need—that was it! Inde-

Mary Claire Kendall, "Was the Tea Party a Success or a Failure in the 2010 Midterm Elections?" *Helium*, November 10, 2010. www.helium.com. Copyright © 2010 by Mary Claire Kendall. All rights reserved. Reproduced by permission of Helium, Inc.

pendent Tea Party–minded Americans bolted—just like early American patriots, who threw out King George's high-tax tea into Boston Harbor.

At town hall after town hall meeting the summer of 2009, Tea Partiers signaled their distaste for Obamacare, that went too far and was too expensive, and their decided yen for that 18th-century Boston Harbor tea party maneuver.

Tea Partiers took [their] anger and resolve all the way to Election Day.

Then, folks like [former Alaskan governor and Republican vice presidential nominee] Sarah Palin, [Representative] Michele Bachmann and Tea Party leaders across the country helped galvanize the movement, giving it a concentrated focus and media attention. It was the Tea Party calling out government as being too fat, too bloated and too cozy with elite, moneyed special interests who engineer deals that benefit themselves but not the broad swath of hardworking Americans who "play by the rules."

Tea Party Anger at the Polls

And, sure enough, independent Tea Partiers took that anger and resolve all the way to Election Day. While 18% of independents voted for Democrats in their takeover of the House and Senate in 2006, 18% of independents swung back and voted for Republicans in their takeover of the House and near-takeover of the Senate in 2010.

Of course, not all the Tea Party–backed candidates won—showing, it's not enough to assert one's determination to get America back on track and back to its roots; you also need to be able to argue your case persuasively. This was particularly true in the Senate races, where candidates like Marco Rubio (R-FL) and Kelly Ayotte (R-NH), strongly backed by the Tea Party, fared well; whereas candidates who sometimes left voters scratching their heads, like Christine O'Donnell (R-DE) and Sharron Angle (R-NV), though very able, came up short on Election Day. In the House, on the other hand, the mood of the country was perfectly reflected in a sea change, bright with red, not seen since World War II. That's exactly how the founders intended it. The House of Representatives was designed to be more responsive to the mood of the country, whereas the Senate would be the less reactive body—putting on the brakes lest the new course proves ultimately misguided.

What a ride—so utterly American! As Santelli said before the very first rally, "I think that this Tea Party phenomenon is steeped in American culture and steeped in the American notion to get involved with what's going on with our government." And, while he didn't do any organizing and had to work during the first Tea Party rally, he said, "I have to tell you—I'm pretty proud of this."

America is too.

The Tea Party Has a Good Chance at Remaining Viable

Justin Quinn

Justin Quinn is a journalist who has worked for several different newspapers in Pennsylvania and Maryland, and who now writes for About.com, a web-based content resource.

The most common word used by political pundits to describe the Tea Party movement is "populist." Does this mean, then, that the Tea Party is an inherently unsustainable movement that will eventually fade into obscurity? If not, how will it retain its independence from outside special interests as it ventures forth into future political campaigns?

Populist, Not Nativist

Senate [Banking, Housing, and Urban Affairs Committee] Chairman Christopher Dodd, who announced his retirement in 2009 after a sudden and disastrous bank failure caused by a sudden and disastrous drop in the housing market, has compared the Tea Party movement to a nativist movement of the mid-nineteenth century known as the "Know Nothing" movement.

While there is little doubt that the Tea Party is indeed a populist movement (meaning it is a bottom-up, grassroots political movement that puts the desires of the ordinary people against the political elites), its nativist ideologies are highly debatable. Nativism is the ideology typically characterized by a fear of or opposition to immigration. The major problem Tea Party members have with immigration reform is the lack of willingness Democratic (and to a lesser extent Republican) leaders have demonstrated to curb *illegal* immigration into the

Justin Quinn, "Is the Tea Party Sustainable?" About.com. Copyright © 2011 Justin Quinn (http://usconservatives.about.com). Used with permission of About, Inc., which can be found online at www.about.com. All rights reserved.

U.S, particularly the flood of Mexican illegals crossing the border into Arizona, California, New Mexico and Texas.

No one can say for sure whether the Tea Party movement is sustainable for the long term, but there are several glaring indications that it is different from other populist movements like the Know Nothings and the Ross Perot movement of the 1990s and has a better chance of remaining viable for years to come.

Tea Party members are typically strongly supportive of big business, an aspect that has opened it up for strong criticism from the Left.

Tea Party Advantages over Other Populist Movements

For example, even though the Tea Party originated with entrenched politicos like former Congressman Dick Armey and political consultant Sal Russo, the movement has attracted everyday Americans disgusted with the ever-expanding reach of government and its appalling spending problem. While the politicos were the ones to get people organized, it wasn't "their" movement. They simply recognized a need for something without a label that needed to unite fiscal conservatives. In most cases, the politicos have ceded the reins to the everyday Americans that now make up the majority of the organizations. Nevertheless, these ties to shrewd political operatives separate the Tea Party from populist movements of the past and ensure its leaders will remain plugged in to the political process for at least the next several years.

Likewise, Tea Party members are typically strongly supportive of big business, an aspect that has opened it up for strong criticism from the Left. Most Tea Partiers, fiscally conservative as they are, are aligned with big *and* small American businesses, believing that only corporate America can get unemployed Americans back to work. In some cases, Tea Party leaders actually consult with representatives from major American companies to help determine policy and endorsements. While the Left is outspoken about the corruptible influence corporations may have on the Tea Party's policy decisions, their leaders are guilty of the same kind of thing; the only difference is that their leaders align themselves with Big Labor instead.

While there can be no guarantees about the future of the Tea Party, being plugged in to the political process and having the financial backing of America's biggest (and smallest) corporations will undoubtedly serve to provide a foundation for the movement that previous populist movements never enjoyed.

Despite the rhetoric from the Left that the Tea Party's affiliation with political players and big business ultimately make it just a tool of the political elites, the movement has managed to retain its autonomy largely because of its very public endorsements and its members' commitment to policing themselves. This much can be attributed to the fact that at its heart, the Tea Party is a true populist movement. The organizations that combine to make up the Tea Party are laid bare when they combine to support a particular candidate. The candidate's background, political positions and overall viability serve as a sort of reflection of the Tea Party movement. If a candidate is a true fiscal conservative, Tea Party members will continue to stay loyal to the cause. If the candidate is in any way unworthy of the endorsement, however, there is little question that Tea Party members will speak up and hold their leaders accountable.

Since it has no official role in government (beyond a Tea Party Caucus established by Republican Congresswoman Michele Bachmann), the Tea Party is free to chart its own course.

Is the Tea Party sustainable? Only time will tell; but it has a better chance than most populist movements.

The Tea Party Is Not a Genuine Political Movement

Stuart Whatley

Stuart Whatley is deputy managing blog editor for the Huffington Post.

Last summer [2009], when mass protests broke out in Iran following what was seen as a rigged election, Americans cried out in support of the uprising through all possible channels. Some commentators here went so far as to claim credit for the "revolution," as if it never could have happened without American political movements having already set the example. But despite the arrogance of that claim, the Iranian Green movement is indeed an exertion of democratic will that resonates closely with many Americans—and for good reason.

America's rich history of successful social and political movements, from its genesis onward, lends profound familiarity to the Iranian uprising, most of which has remained nonviolent. The enduring American symbolic identity—as a bastion of freedom and opportunity—is mostly justified when one considers the relative success of the civil rights or feminist movements of the 20th century, or of the ongoing LGBT [lesbian, gay, bisexual, and transgender] rights movement, which continues to make incremental gains today. American democracy, fueled by an active populace—despite its numerous imperfections—remains the gold standard around the world.

It is against this venerable historical backdrop that one must concede that the most well-known, highly publicized American social/political movement today—the Tea Party movement—is a national embarrassment.

Stuart Whatley, "The Tea Party Movement Is a National Embarrassment," *Huffington Post*, February 9, 2010. Copyright © 2010 by Stuart Whatley. All rights reserved. Reproduced by permission of the author.

An Illegitimate Movement

At its core, the Tea Party movement is rife with contradiction, incoherence and a willful contempt for facts or reason. It is but a parody of the legitimate movements for which American democracy has historically been held in such high regard. It is, in fact, the latest installment in quite another American tradition: the exploitation of frustrated, desperate, and susceptible people by monied interests and profiteers.

The impetus for the civil rights movement was centuries of racially based oppression at all levels of American government and society. The logic behind its call for equality was overwhelming. Now consider the Tea Party movement, whose foremost demand of a president who in his first month passed one of the biggest tax cuts ever ... is for tax cuts. The movement's incoherence is only illuminated further when this demand is uttered in the same sentence as its call for deficit reduction.

The Tea Party movement—is a national embarrassment.

Though the movement claims to have no defined leadership, there are public figures and entities who nevertheless carry that mantle, which has led to perhaps its greatest irony: a portion of the American populace who carries a populist banner against the coddling of greedy bankers is led by some of the country's most cynical and base profiteers.

When the movement was christened last April for a large tax day protest, it was derived wholesale from the efforts of a registered corporate lobbyist and a right-leaning cable news network, whose president recently pointed out that it's all about ratings. At the Tea Party's national convention last weekend [February 4, 2010], its keynote speaker was a former governor [Sarah Palin] who quit midterm in order to peddle a book that she didn't write, but for which she collects most of the royalties. If this were Iran's Green movement, these would be the people slinging marked-up green headbands on the street corner.

Of course, the Tea Party is not without its whistleblowers. The $500 per plate entry fee to last week's convention almost led to it being canceled altogether. But the exodus of reasonable elements will only homogenize the movement further towards a particularly polarizing worldview that opens itself to continued profit-driven exploitation.

An Authoritarian Worldview

In *Authoritarianism & Polarization in American Politics*, a revealing work of political science published last year that unfortunately went somewhat unnoticed, Marc J. Hetherington and Jonathan D. Weiler describe a specific worldview—*authoritarianism*—which they argue lies at the heart of political polarization in modern American politics. (It should be noted: Their use of the term "authoritarian" is not related to the more quotidian and overly negative connotation associated with despotic regimes; rather, it describes a particular lens through which certain people view the world, based on a wide range of scholarly work spanning the fields of psychology, sociology, political science, and other cognitive sciences.)

According to Hetherington and Weiler, authoritarians tend to rely more on emotion and instinct in decision making, view politics in black and white, resent confusion or ambiguity in the social order, and are suspicious of specific groups who they believe could alter that order (typically gays and immigrants). The difference between authoritarians and nonauthoritarians, according to the authors, becomes far more pronounced during tumultuous economic or social periods when there are more perceived "threats." During such times, authoritarians in particular lose accuracy motivation and, "become much less interested than nonauthoritarians in seeking information that [is] balanced in its approach, and much more interested in pursuing one-sided information that reinforc[es] existing beliefs." Or in other words, they are highly susceptible to misinformation campaigns, the likes of which pervaded the health care reform debate last summer.

[The Tea Party] is loud, passionate, and generally unconcerned with pesky things like facts or reasoned, practical solutions to the country's problems.

Most every characteristic of an authoritarian worldview lends itself well to the impassioned rhetoric of the Tea Party movement and to the shrewd players operating behind the scenes and atop the soap box. The movement's overly simplified, often-confused solutions to complex problems align with authoritarians' Manichean [believing in religious or philosophical dualism] worldview. That [former Republican congressman] Tom Tancredo's anti-immigrant laced speech at last weekend's convention was well received comes as no surprise. And that this is the group who so often embraces proven falsehoods and spin-narratives to defend its anti-administration agenda should speak for itself with regards to accuracy motivation.

Despite the criticism it receives, the Tea Party continues to be praised as a political force. It is loud, passionate, and generally unconcerned with pesky things like facts or reasoned, practical solutions to the country's problems. This bodes ill for 2010's political environment, and it is a shameful representation of what constitutes an American political or social movement. While the Tea Party may alienate some who see it for the profit machine that it is, others who share the fearful, intolerant authoritarian worldview that it is increasingly coalescing around will be lured in and pitted against the very people in power who could actually help them. That this movement has grown political legs is too bad, and by Hetherington and Weiler's account, it means even more polarization is yet to come.

The Tea Party's Importance Has Been Exaggerated

Stephanie Mencimer

Stephanie Mencimer is a reporter for the Washington bureau of the progressive political magazine Mother Jones.

The Tea Party lost the food fight. Despite opposition from conservative activists, including the professional lobbyists at FreedomWorks [a conservative political group], the Senate passed a landmark food safety bill 73 to 25 on Tuesday [November 31, 2010] that would give the federal government broad new powers to police the food system. The vote, a rare display of bipartisanship, virtually assures that President [Barack] Obama will be able to sign the bill before Americans carve up their Christmas goose.

Tea Party Weakness in Fighting Legislation

Not too much should be read into any one political act, but the failure of the Tea Party to derail the legislation is significant—perhaps a sign that the movement has been given too much credit as a political power broker. Tea Party activists have been vocal and have focused politicians' attention on fiscal issues like the deficit. And to be sure, the Tea Partiers helped get out the vote for Republican candidates. But in many cases, they only succeeded in electing candidates who were also heavily backed by corporate interests. More than 60 percent of Tea Party candidates lost their races. Those who won were people like multimillionaire Ron Johnson, who defeated progressive Democrat Sen. Russ Feingold in Wisconsin. But Feingold was also heavily targeted by the US Chamber of

Adapted from an article by Stephanie Mencimer, "How Powerful Is the Tea Party Anyway?" *Mother Jones*, December 1, 2010. www.motherjones.com. Copyright © 2010, Foundation for National Progress. All rights reserved. Reproduced by permission of Mother Jones.

Commerce and other corporate interests who hated his stands on everything from mandatory arbitration to campaign finance reform. Outside groups spent at least $5 million to help defeat Feingold, making it tough to attribute Johnson's victory to Tea Party organizing.

> *The failure of the Tea Party to derail the [food safety] legislation is significant—perhaps a sign that the movement has been given too much credit as a political power broker.*

If the food safety vote [December 2010 congressional vote to approve sweeping changes in regulating food safety] is any indication, a similar dynamic may be at work regarding the Tea Party's legislative agenda. Food safety may simply be an issue that doesn't get Tea Party activists frothing the way, say, health care reform or auditing the Fed [the Federal Reserve, the nation's central bank] do. But what's more likely is that the Tea Party is no more effective in fighting corporate interests than MoveOn [a progressive political group]. And the vast majority of the food industry backed this bill. Poisoning customers, as it turns out, is very expensive and especially bad for business. Big Ag [the agriculture industry] and the food processors decided that if they were going to do something about the problem, it would be a lot cheaper to let the taxpayers pay for food inspections rather than foot the tab themselves, and they got behind the bill. Not even [conservative commentator] Glenn Beck could rally enough Tea Party opposition to kill it. On the day of the vote, Beck urged his millions of viewers and listeners to oppose the measure. But it passed by a wide margin, with 15 GOP [Republican] votes, including those of newly sworn-in Illinois Sen. Mark Kirk, who beat a Tea Party candidate in the GOP primary.

Just as Tea Party candidates don't win elections without corporate backing, when the Tea Party is pressed into battle against big business, it usually loses. That's what happened with the health care debate. Despite the massive protests—such as the angry showings at packed town hall meetings in the summer of 2009—all the Tea Party fist-waving failed to stop the bill's passage. True, the Democrats had control of both the House and Senate, but that has never guaranteed progress on health care in the past. The difference this time around was that the Obama administration successfully bought off many of the special health care interests that might have otherwise fought the bill. The drug companies, the powerful American Medical Association, and much of the insurance industry were instead sitting at the table, rather, than lobbying to kill the bill outright.

A Threat to Moderates

That's not to dismiss the movement entirely, of course. The Tea Party has some influence, but only under the right and increasingly limited conditions, such as with vulnerable moderate Republicans. As my colleague [reporter] Suzy Khimm elaborates on . . . Sen. Olympia Snowe, the moderate Republican from Maine, switched her stance on earmarks this week, voting Tuesday in favor of an earmark moratorium amendment. (The amendment ultimately failed.) In March, Snowe voted against a moratorium. Khimm attributes the change to the Tea Party's threat to challenge her in the GOP primary in 2012. And earlier this month, after Glenn Beck erroneously reported that Sen. Orrin Hatch (R-Utah) had voted to advance the food safety bill, Tea Partiers got fired up enough that Hatch posted a column on Beck's website emphasizing that he did indeed oppose the bill. (Hatch's colleague from Utah, Robert Bennett was unexpectedly ousted in the GOP primary this year with help from Tea Party activists, many of whom see Hatch as their next target.)

But in general, the Tea Party movement has only been truly successful when its interests align with corporate

America's. Whether their agenda is praiseworthy or not, the Tea Partiers have shown a commitment to working through the democratic process to achieve their goals, successfully mobilizing thousands of people who, up until then, hadn't been very politically engaged. Yet when it comes to real, from-the-ground-up change, even the Tea Partiers can't usually pull it off. Perhaps that's a good thing: Letting a small group of angry people direct policy changes from one year to the next isn't exactly a formula for a stable democracy. At the same time, however, it means that corporate money really does have a choke hold on the political system, and even the angriest and most organized of grassroots activists aren't going to do much to change that.

The Tea Party Is a Movement Funded and Exploited by Corporations

Larisa Alexandrovna

Larisa Alexandrovna is an investigative journalist and writer who contributes to numerous websites and publications.

Yes, we really do need a third party in this country (and then some). But a party of Birthers [people who question whether President Barack Obama was born in the United States] who don't know the basics of American history?

"But this past weekend [February 4, 2010] in Nashville, at the first National Tea Party Convention, the Beltway press did just the opposite with regard to [former Alaska governor and vice presidential nominee] Sarah Palin's keynote address, which *did* follow a prime-time speech by "birther" nut Joseph Farah, who over the years *has* carved out a uniquely hateful and demented corner of the right-wing blogosphere. Because, yes, at the Tea Party convention, Farah, a proud Muslim-hater and gay-hater, *did* receive a standing ovation from the conservative crowd after he unfurled his thoroughly debunked birther garbage (i.e., Obama "doesn't have a birth certificate"). And Farah *did* brag in the weeks leading up to the event about his chance to share the stage with Palin, to associate with Palin. ("Sold Out! Palin-Farah Ticket Rocks Tea Party Convention," read the headline at Farah's discredited right-wing site, WorldNetDaily.com.)

Worst of all, though, the press played dumb about the whole thing.

Fact: Virtually nobody in the corporate media said boo about Palin helping to legitimize Farah by sharing the same stage with him. She was given a total free ride."

Larisa Alexandrovna, "Corporate Funded, Conspiracy Sniffing, Revolutionaries ...," At Largely, February 10, 2010. www.atlargely.com. Copyright © 2010 by Larisa Alexandrovna. All rights reserved. Reproduced by permission of the author.

The Tea Party Movement

And they are educated on American history too:

> "The Tea Party movement has no leader. But it does have a face: William Temple of Brunswick, Ga. For months, the amiable middle-aged activist has been crisscrossing America, appearing at Tea Party events dressed in his trademark three-cornered hat and Revolutionary garb. When journalists interview him (which is often—his outfit draws them in like a magnet), he presents himself as a human bridge between the founders' era and our own. "We fought the British over a 3 percent tea tax. We might as well bring the British back," he told NPR [National Public Radio] during a recent protest outside the Capitol."

A Corporate-Funded Movement

Okay class, one more time—what was the Boston Tea Party about? While it is true that the Boston Tea Party was part of a larger effort aimed at the British monarchy, the colonists knew that the real power was held in the hands of companies:

> The Boston Tea Party arose from two issues confronting the British Empire in 1773: the financial problems of the British East India Company, and an ongoing dispute about the extent of Parliament's authority, if any, over the British American colonies without seating any elected representation. The North Ministry's attempt to resolve these issues produced a showdown that would eventually result in revolution.

The current Tea Party is a movement funded by corporations, which then use their members as protest weapons against their own interests.

Consider the actions the colonists took against the British East India Company, which—like our corporations—had a very special status:

> The East India Company (also the East India Trading Company, English East India Company, and then the British East

India Company) was an early English joint-stock company that was formed initially for pursuing trade with the East Indies, but that ended up trading mainly with the Indian subcontinent and China.

The company long held a privileged position in relation to the English, and later the British, government. As a result, it was frequently granted special rights and privileges, including trade monopolies and exemptions. These caused resentment among its competitors, who saw unfair advantage in the company's position. Despite this resentment, the company remained a powerful force for over 200 years over India.

The final standoff was the destruction of corporate property—tea—which in current times would be called terrorism. Now if this new Tea Party movement actually were like our Founding Fathers, they would be destroying the property of banks and so forth, and even dumping oil. I may not agree with them, but at least they would be true to the name of their movement.

Instead, the current Tea Party is a movement funded by corporations, which then use their members as protest weapons against their own interests. In other words, the current Tea Party movement is made up of the complete antithesis to the principles of our Founding Fathers and are stupid enough to be used as pawns by the very people they should be targeting.

If these people would protest on Wall Street instead of the idiocy we are now watching, I would easily join them. But if I showed up to protest Wall Street and demand that corporate control of our government be eliminated, I would be called a Commie [Communist], a terrorist, and all sorts of neat little non-applicable names.

Most American Voters Oppose the Tea Party as a Third Party

Sean J. Miller

Sean J. Miller is a reporter for the Hill, *a daily congressional newspaper and website.*

A majority of likely voters think a viable third party would be good for American politics, according to a new poll of likely voters in 10 key open House districts.

Those voters are split, however, on whether the Tea Party should be that alternative.

Support for a Third Party

Fifty-four percent of respondents in the *Hill* 2010 Midterm Election Poll said they'd like an alternative to the Democrats and Republicans.

That number rose to 67 percent for self-identified independents. But even a plurality in the established parties—49 percent of Democrats and 46 percent of Republicans—said they'd like another choice.

"That's probably the strongest number I've seen in a poll of people in America saying that they're interested in a third party," said pollster Mark Penn.

"There's a record number of independents and a record number of people looking for a possible third party," he said. "And that's a big finding. There's an opportunity here."

The *Hill*'s poll was conducted by Penn Schoen Berland, which surveyed 4,047 likely voters in 10 open districts. The overall sample has a margin of error of plus or minus 1.5 percent.

Sean J. Miller, "POLL: Majority of Voters Say They Want a Viable Third Party in American Politics," *The Hill*, October 13, 2010. www.thehill.com. Copyright © 2010 by Sean J. Miller. All rights reserved. Reproduced by permission of Featurewell.com, Inc.

"I think there's a greater potential for a third party than perhaps [at] any time in our history," said Mark McKinnon, a Republican strategist and former adviser to George W. Bush. "There is a very broad level of dissatisfaction throughout the electorate—right, left and middle.

"I think what's happened goes beyond general dissatisfaction with the economy," he added. "They want a new way—they want to feel empowered again."

Fifty-four percent of respondents in the Hill *2010 Midterm Election Poll said they'd like an alternative to the Democrats and Republicans.*

The Tea Party as a Third Party

The rise of the Tea Party movement—a mishmash of disparate organizations under one umbrella—serves as one of the strongest signals that the public is dissatisfied with Democratic and Republican government. But asked if they thought the Tea Party should be the new third party, voters divided. More than two-thirds of Democrats and 42 percent of independents said no. But 55 percent of Republicans said yes, which is perhaps a sign of dissatisfaction among rank-and-file GOPers [Republicans], and also an acknowledgement that the Tea Party is fueling what appears to be a Republican wave this cycle.

McKinnon said the Tea Party movement is just the "tip of the spear" in the push for a third party.

"They've just unlocked the door," he said. "And voters are kicking the door open."

The next presidential election, in 2012, could see a third-party contender, McKinnon noted.

"I think, professionally speaking, it's more likely to happen in a presidential year."

Several third parties have risen to prominence, most notably as spoilers in presidential elections. In 1912, former President Theodore Roosevelt made an unsuccessful bid to reclaim the White House by running on the Progressive ticket.

More recently, Ross Perot ran under the Reform Party banner vote in the 1992 presidential election, capturing almost 20 percent of the popular vote, which helped Bill Clinton topple President George H.W. Bush.

> *More than two-thirds of Democrats and 42 percent of independents said no [to the Tea Party as a third party]. But 55 percent of Republicans said yes.*

Ralph Nader made several presidential runs as a Green Party candidate, but his most notable feat was siphoning votes away from Vice President Al Gore in 2000. Rep. Ron Paul (R-Texas) and others have also made runs for the presidency—with modest success—under the Libertarian Party banner.

Third Parties Present Too Many Unknowns

For a third party to arise, it would need to be driven by a compelling personality, according to Ross Baker, a political science professor at Rutgers University.

"If there were a single individual identified with the third party—a Teddy Roosevelt, a Ross Perot—you would have a personality to attract people," he said.

Baker doubted a third-party candidate could capture the White House—or even win a typical congressional race.

"At the presidential level, historically, they're spoilers," Baker explained. "At the state level, less so, because people are much more dependent on party label to make a decision. The information level is very low—so as a consequence, [third parties] don't have much of an impact.

"The franchise matters. It gives people voting cues when there's no other information available."

Baker said he doubted the Tea Party would ever become a viable political party. "You vote for a Democrat, a Republican, you know what you're getting. You vote for a Tea Party person, you could be getting a pig in a poke," he said.

Taking Over the Republican Party

Tea Party activists say their movement is unwilling to be co-opted into the traditional party structure anyway.

"Not only no, but hell no," Judson Phillips, the founder of the group Tea Party Nation, said when asked about the prospect of forming a third party.

"Third parties are simply an invitation to disaster," he said. "All a third party does is split the vote. "I am yet to meet anyone who wants to have the Tea Party as a [political party]," he said—the more appealing prospect is to "take over" the Republican Party.

The Tea Party Nation organized a national conference in Nashville in February [2010] and had one planned for October in Las Vegas. But in a sign of how difficult it is to sustain such a disparate grassroots movement, the Las Vegas conference was called off.

"People weren't willing to buy tickets," Phillips said. "We just didn't have the drive that we had for the first one."

Meanwhile, McKinnon pointed to the unpredictability of the U.S. political system as one reason why the launch of a third party shouldn't be discounted.

"The great thing about American politics is we turn conventional wisdom on its ear," he said.

CHAPTER 2

Is the Tea Party Movement Racist?

Chapter Preface

The Tea Party has been criticized for being a political movement composed of mostly Caucasian Americans, but one of the Tea Party's strongest supporters is an African American from South Carolina—Tim Scott. A Republican and former insurance agent, Scott was elected to the US House of Representatives in 2010 from one of the most conservative districts in South Carolina, after defeating Paul Thurmond, the son of the legendary segregationist Senator Strom Thurmond. Scott's win made him the first African American Republican to be elected to Congress from the Deep South since Reconstruction and the first African American Republican elected to the US Congress since J.C. Watts in 2003. Scott won his Senate race with a strong showing—by capturing 69 percent of the vote in a runoff election.

Tim Scott ran on a Tea Party platform and received endorsements from many Tea Party activists, including Sarah Palin. In his campaign, Scott emphasized Tea Party values such as fiscal restraint, low taxes, and smaller government. He criticized Democrats as socialists whose big spending ideas will only increase the national debt. Scott promised voters that he would not support any type of spending that adds to the deficit and that he would oppose earmarks—legislative provisions that allocate money for special purposes, usually pet projects of individual legislators. He also pledged not to serve more than four terms. As a die-hard conservative, Scott also embraced other right-wing Republican positions. He supported the military's "don't ask, don't tell" policy for dealing with homosexuals (a policy rejected by the lame-duck 2010 Congress), and he opposes same-sex marriage. Scott also vowed to oppose cap-and-trade climate legislation and amnesty for illegal immigrants, and to seek repeal of President Barack Obama's health care law—one of the first agenda items of the Tea Party.

In interviews, Scott has said that his election victory shows that Tea Party conservatives do not care about the color of a person's skin but rather about political ideas and ideals. Indeed, Scott received the votes of many white South Carolina citizens due to his embrace of Tea Party principles. Scott's victory contradicts the view expressed by many commentators who have suggested that the Tea Party's opposition to President Barack Obama is racially based.

Tim Scott, however, is not very popular among African Americans, many of whom tend to vote for Democrats and strongly disagree with conservative values. Scott, for his part, does not seek the approval of other African Americans, and he does not like to be identified by race. When asked about the historical significance of his win, Scott downplays the racial angle. After he was elected, he also refused to join the Congressional Black Caucus, a group of African American congressmen and women. Instead, he is a promoter of Tea Party and conservative causes, which he sees as essential to restraining the federal government.

Many political commentators say that Tim Scott's election provides insight into the Tea Party mind-set on race. The viewpoints in this chapter address the critical issue of whether the Tea Party is racist, either overtly or in more subtle ways.

Tea Party Activists Include White Nationalists and Other Racists

Bill Berkowitz

Bill Berkowitz is a contributing writer to the Global Issues website and a longtime observer of the conservative movement.

It began with Apr. 15 Tax Day protests as thousands rallied in a number of cities across the country.

It continued on into the summer with raucous town hall meetings and gun-toting anti-Barack Obama demonstrators, and appeared to reach its apex with a Sep. 12 march on Washington, which drew nearly 100,000 participants.

Now, however, some in the so-called Tea Party movement are turning their attention toward becoming a force during the 2010 congressional elections.

Several reports on the Sep. 12 event noted it was a nearly all-white crowd and some demonstrators carried an assortment of 'homemade' anti-Obama posters, declaring that 'The Anti-Christ Is Living in the White House', and calling the president an 'Oppressive Bloodsucking Arrogant Muslim Alien'.

Despite the fact that it doesn't have a clear identity, and serious questions about the movement's character remain to be answered, the Tea Party movement has been one of the most intriguing political developments of the past year.

Is it a grassroots movement, or has it been organised and funded by Washington-based conservative groups? Could it be both? Is it mainly concerned with economic issues (government spending, taxes, deficits) or are the Christian Right's traditional social issues (abortion, same-sex marriage) of interest to Tea Partiers?

Bill Berkowitz, "U.S.: White Supremacists Crash Anti-Obama Tea Party," Global Issues, December 22, 2009. www.globalissues.org. Copyright © 2009 by Bill Berkowitz. All rights reserved. Reproduced by permission of Inter Press Service.

Are there several—possibly competing—ideological tendencies within the movement?

While Tea Partiers made a lot of noise this past summer, doing their best to put the kybosh on health care reform, is there a future for the movement?

A recent Rasmussen poll suggests that there very well might be.

In theoretical three-way congressional races between a Democrat, Republican and Tea Party candidate, the Tea Party candidate outpolled the Republican. Democrats attracted 36 percent of the vote; the Tea Party candidate received 23 percent, and the Republican finished third at 18 percent, with 22 percent undecided.

(According to the Rasmussen Reports website, 'survey ... respondents were asked to assume that the Tea Party movement organized as a new political party. In practical terms, it is unlikely that a true third-party option would perform as well as the polling data indicates. The rules of the election process—written by Republicans and Democrats—provide substantial advantages for the two established major parties.)

While Tea Party events have become a safe haven for people carrying racist anti-Obama signs, people of colour have stayed away in droves.

Interestingly enough, in an effort to build the movement, some Tea Party organisers have taken to 'studying the grassroots training methods of the late Saul Alinsky, the community organizer known for campus protests in the 1960s and who inspired the structure of Obama's presidential campaign,' the *San Francisco Chronicle* recently reported.

Tea Party groups are also using *Tea Party: The Documentary Film* as an organising tool. In a pre-premiere press release, the filmmakers claimed that the film would deal with the 'allegations of racism'.

Is the Tea Party Movement Racist?

And that indeed appears to be the issue that could stymie the movement's growth.

While Tea Party events have become a safe haven for people carrying racist anti-Obama signs, people of colour have stayed away in droves. Members of white nationalist organisations openly participate in Tea Party events and view the movement as a fertile recruiting ground.

Questions about the overlap between Tea Partiers and anti-immigration activists might be answered when an immigration reform bill is taken up next year.

Are the openly racist elements within the Tea Party movement an aberration scorned by most Tea Party participants as John Hawkins, who runs a website called Right Wing News, insists, or are they more firmly entrenched than Tea Partiers would care to admit?

'The tea parties themselves are made up of a diverse bloc of different political elements, and white nationalists have chosen to make a stand inside the tea parties,' one expert, Devin Burghart, told IPS.

For the past 17 years, Burghart has researched and written on virtually all facets of contemporary white nationalism. He is currently vice president of the Institute for Research & Education on Human Rights, which monitors and publishes on the activities of white nationalist groups.

'The exact extent of the racist element inside the tea parties is difficult to quantify, because they are not a static phenomena, and it depends on who shows up,' he explained, 'That said, it's enough of a factor to attract the attention of a significant portion of the white nationalist movement.'

'It's not a matter of how many African-American or Latino/a folks show up at these tea parties, it's about the content and character of the arguments made at them,' Burghart added.

Not only have 'Tea Partiers turned up with overtly racist signs and slogans' at rallies from coast to coast, he said, but also many participants 'cling to the belief that our first African-American president is not only un-American, he was not even born in the country'.

Unfortunately, Burghart noted, 'There's little evidence to indicate that Tea Party leaders are doing anything to address the racism in their ranks.'

Burghart said that he was not surprised that 'Tea Party activists would deny their racism'. After all, 'racists have been denying their racism even before pro-secessionist bigots couched their arguments in bogus claims about states' rights'.

However, he added, 'To anyone with any degree of sensitivity to the issue, the Tea Partiers have clearly shown themselves to be racist, in the lineage of George Wallace—who when he campaigned up North eschewed talk of racial segregation in favour ranting against elites.'

In an article at the Institute for Research & Education on Human Rights' website, Leonard Zeskind, the organisation's president and author of the recently published *Blood and Politics: The History of White Nationalism from the Margins to the Mainstream*, pointed out that the anti-Obama 'opposition' contains 'many different political elements'.

If Tea Party activists can ferret out racists and white nationalists from their ranks ... [the Tea Party] could become a legitimate force on the US political landscape.

These include 'ultra-conservative Republicans of both the Pat Buchanan and free market variety; anti-tax Tea Party Libertarians from the Ron Paul camp; Christian Right activists intent on re-molding the country into their kind of kingdom; birth certificate conspiracy theorists, anti-immigrant nativists of the armed Minuteman and the policy wonk variety; third party "constitutionalists"; and white nationalists of both the citizens councils and the Stormfront national socialist variety.'

If Tea Party activists can ferret out racists and white nationalists from their ranks—and not become a mouthpiece for Christian Right ideologues—it could become a legitimate force on the US political landscape.

Meanwhile, a host of groups, operating under assorted Tea Party banners, are working to influence the 2010 midterm elections.

Tea Party Supporters Are Upset About a Black President

Eugene Robinson

Eugene Robinson is an associate editor and twice-weekly columnist for the Washington Post, *a daily newspaper published in Washington, DC.*

The first African-American president takes office, and almost immediately we see the birth of a big, passionate national movement—overwhelmingly white and lavishly funded—that tries its best to delegitimize that president, seeks to thwart his every initiative, and manages to bring the discredited and moribund opposition party roaring back to life. Coincidence?

Not a chance. But also not that simple.

First, I'll state the obvious: It's not racist to criticize President [Barack] Obama, it's not racist to have conservative views, and it's not racist to join the Tea Party. But there's something about the nature and tone of the most vitriolic attacks on the president that I believe is distinctive—and difficult to explain without asking whether race is playing a role.

"Taking Government Back" Rhetoric

One thing that struck me from the beginning about the Tea Party rhetoric is the idea of reclaiming something that has been taken away.

At a recent campaign rally in Paducah, Ky., Senate candidate Rand Paul, a darling of the Tea Party movement, drew thunderous applause when he said that if Republicans win, "we get to go to Washington and take back our government."

Eugene Robinson, "Racism and the Tea Party Movement," *Washington Post*, November 2, 2010. Copyright © 2010 The Washington Post. All rights reserved. Used by permission and protected by the Copyright Laws of the United States. The printing, copying, redistribution, or retransmission of the Material without express written permission is prohibited.

Take it back from whom? Maybe he thinks it goes without saying, because he didn't say.

On Sunday, in a last-minute fund-raising appeal, Republican presidential hopeful Mike Huckabee implored his supporters to help "return American government to the American people."

Again, who's in possession of the government right now, if not the American people? The non-American people? The un-American people?

There's an obvious answer, but it's one that generally comes from the progressive end of the political spectrum: Americans must fight to take back their government from the lobbyists and big-money special interests that shape our laws to suit their own interests, not for the good of the nation.

That may be what some Tea Partiers have in mind, but the movement hasn't seen fit to make campaign finance reform one of its major issues. And the establishment Republicans who are surfing the Tea Party wave—while at the same time scheming to co-opt the movement—would view the idea of taking money out of politics with horror, if they thought it might actually happen.

Suspicions About a Black President

So who stole the government? What makes some people feel more disenfranchised now than they were, say, during the presidency of George W. Bush?

After all, it was Bush who inherited a budget surplus and left behind a suffocating deficit—I'm not being tendentious, just stating the facts. It was Bush who launched two wars without making any provision in the budget to pay for them, who proposed and won an expensive new prescription-drug entitlement without paying for it, who bailed out irresponsible Wall Street firms with the $700 billion TARP [Troubled Asset Relief Program].

Bush was vilified by critics while he was in office, but not with the suggestion that somehow the government had been seized or usurped—that it had fallen into hands that were not those of "the American people." Yet this is the Tea Party suggestion about Obama.

I ask myself what's so different about Obama, and the answer is pretty obvious: He's black.

Underlying all the Tea Party's issues and complaints, it appears to me, is the entirely legitimate issue of the relationship between the individual and the federal government. But why would this concern about oppressive, intrusive government become so acute now? Why didn't, say, government surveillance of domestic phone calls and e-mails get the constitutional fundamentalists all worked up?

I have to wonder what it is about Obama that provokes and sustains all this Tea Party ire. I wonder how he can be seen as "elitist," when he grew up in modest circumstances—his mother was on food stamps for a time—and paid for his fancy-pants education with student loans. I wonder how people who genuinely cherish the American dream can look at a man who lived that dream and feel no connection, no empathy.

I ask myself what's so different about Obama, and the answer is pretty obvious: He's black. For whatever reason, I think this makes some people unsettled, anxious, even suspicious—witness the willingness of so many to believe absurd conspiracy theories about Obama's birthplace, his religion, and even his absent father's supposed Svengali-like influence from the grave.

Obama has made mistakes that rightly cost him political support. But I can't help believing that the Tea Party's rise was partly due to circumstances beyond his control—that he's different from other presidents, and that the difference is his race.

The Tea Party Is All About Race

Bob Cesca

Bob Cesca is an author, screenwriter, director, and producer, as well as a featured contributor to the Huffington Post.

I was going to open this [viewpoint] with an analogy about the Tea Party groups and why they're treated seriously by the press and the Republicans. The analogy would go something like: "Imagine [insert left-wing activist group here] getting a serious profile in a mainstream newspaper, and imagine serious Democratic politicians appearing at their convention."

The problem is, when I really evaluated what the various Far-Left activist groups are all about and compared them with the Tea Party movement, there really wasn't any equivalency. At all.

Because when you strip away all of the rage, all of the nonsensical loud noises and all of the contradictions, all that's left is race. The Tea Party is almost entirely about race, and there's no comparative group on the left that's similarly motivated by bigotry, ignorance and racial hatred.

Real Racism

I hasten to note that I'm talking about *real racism*, insofar as it's impossible for the majority race—the 70 percent white majority—to be on the receiving end of racism. That is unless white males, for example, are suddenly an oppressed racial demographic. But judging by the racial composition of, say, the Senate or AM talk radio or the cast members playing the Obamas on SNL [*Saturday Night Live*, a late-night variety show], I don't think white people have anything to worry about.

Bob Cesca, "The Tea Party Is All About Race," *Huffington Post*, March 3, 2010. www.huffingtonpost.com. Copyright © 2010 by Bob Cesca. All rights reserved. Reproduced by permission of the author.

This isn't an epiphany by any stretch. From the beginning, with their witch doctor imagery, watermelon agitprop and Curious George effigies, the wing-nut Right has been dying to blurt out, as Lee Atwater [Republican political strategist] famously said "n-----, n-----, n-----!"

But they can't.

Strike that. Correction. TeaParty.org founder Dale Robertson brandished a sign with the (misspelled) word "n---a-." So they're not even as restrained as the generally unstrung Atwater anymore.

Most of the time, they merely *imply* the use of the word. [Conservative talk radio personality] Rush Limbaugh referring to the president as a "black man-child," for example. Every week, a new example pops up on the radio and somehow the offenders are able to keep their jobs while [radio celebrity] Howard Stern is fined for saying the comparatively innocuous word "blumpkin." Limbaugh, on the other hand, can stoke racial animosity on his show by suggesting that health care reform is a civil rights bill—reparations—and no one seems to mind. And no, the impotence isn't an adequate karmic punishment for Limbaugh's roster of trespasses.

The Tea Party is an extension of talk radio. It's an extension of Fox News Channel. It's an extension of the southern faction of the Republican Party—the faction that gave us the Southern Strategy,[1] the Willie Horton ad,[2] the White Hands ad[3] and the racially divisive politics of [political advisors] Lee

---

1. The Southern Strategy was a political strategy employed during the late twentieth century by Republican political campaigns that exploited racist fears among white voters in the South.
2. The Willie Horton ad was run during the 1988 US presidential campaign of George H.W. Bush who criticized his opponent, Democratic governor of Massachusetts Michael Dukakis, for supporting the weekend furlough program that allowed convicted murderer Willie Horton to be released and commit further crimes.
3. The White Hands ad was run during the 1990 North Carolina Senate race between Republican Jesse Helms and his challenger, Democratic and African American candidate Harvey Gantt, and showed a pair of Caucasian hands crumpling a job application rejection while a voice states, "You needed that job, but they had to give it to a minority."

Atwater and Karl Rove. It's an extension of the race-baiting and, often, the outright racism evident in all of those conservative spheres.

Subtle Racism

But unlike the heavy-handedness of Dale Robertson and others, the Tea Party followers are generally more veiled about why they're so outraged by our current president.

In the *New York Times* this past weekend [March 2010], David Barstow profiled a teabagger [pejorative term for Tea Party member] from Idaho:

> SANDPOINT, Idaho—Pam Stout has not always lived in fear of her government. She remembers her years working in federal housing programs, watching the government lift struggling families with job training and education. She beams at the memory of helping a Vietnamese woman get into junior college.
>
> But all that was before the Great Recession and the bank bailouts, before Barack Obama took the White House by promising sweeping change on multiple fronts, before her son lost his job and his house. Mrs. Stout said she awoke to see Washington as a threat, a place where crisis is manipulated—even manufactured—by both parties to grab power.

Now you might be saying to yourself, *I don't see the racism here*. But if you eliminate all of the reasons for Stout's participation in the Tea Party movement as being contradictory or nonsensical, all that's left is race.

Let's deconstruct.

She claims to be against the bank bailouts, but the Tea Party is against the president's bank fee designed to recover the TARP [Troubled Asset Relief Program] money. They also appear to be against financial regulatory reform. None of this makes any sense. If Tea Partiers are against the bailouts, basic logic dictates that they ought to be in favor of getting the

Is the Tea Party Movement Racist?

money back. Or do they prefer that the banks keep the money and orchestrate further meltdowns? Honestly, I'm not even entirely sure they realize that the bailouts and the recovery act (stimulus) are two different things. But they're also against the recovery act—you know, whatever *that* is.

She also told the *New York Times* that she's tired of politicians "manufacturing crisis."

Right. Three things here.

First, where was she—where were the teabaggers—when the Far Right endorsed and supported a massive increase in the size of government, unitary executive power grabs and unconstitutional measures fueled by fearmongering over the very remote threat of terrorism? Crickets chirping. The odds of being killed in an airborne terrorist attack are literally 1 in 10 million. You're much more likely to kill *yourself* than to be killed by a terrorist.

Second, I refuse to believe that health care is a "manufactured crisis." People are going broke and dying every day. Even the most conservative estimates show that there are 9/11-level [referring to the September 11, 2001, attacks on the United States] casualties each month due to a lack of adequate health insurance. The horror stories are readily available online. Just Google "health insurance horror story" and see how manufactured the crisis is.

There's no other way to explain why [Tea Party supporters] ... only decided to collectively freak out when this "foreign" and "exotic" president [Barack Obama] came along.

Third, look at any bar graph of the economy as of one year ago or any basic jobs number and tell me if the crisis is manufactured. Hell, Pam Stout's son lost his house! How can she possibly suggest the economic crisis was manufactured?

I hate to single out one person, but Stout's incongruous anger is indicative of the entire movement.

Fear of a Black President

From the outset, the Tea Party was based on a contradictory premise (the original [Boston] Tea Party was a protest against a corporate tax cut). And when you throw out all of the nonsense and contradictions, there's nothing left except race. There's no other way to explain why these people were silent and compliant for so long, and only decided to collectively freak out when this "foreign" and "exotic" president came along and, right out of the chute, passed the *largest middle-class tax cut in American history*—something they would otherwise support, for goodness sake, it was $288 billion in tax cuts!—we're left to deduce no other motive but the ugly one that lurks just beneath the pale flesh, the tri-corner hats and the dangly tea bag ornamentation.

Irrespective of whether the president passed a huge tax cut or went out of his way to bring Republicans into the health care process, the seeds of racial animosity from the Far Right were sown during the campaign. In those lines waiting for then vice presidential candidate and current Tea Party heroine Sarah Palin, their loud noises spread the pre-scripted lies, lies that entirely hinged on the president's African heritage. A white candidate would never be accused of being a secret Muslim. A white candidate would never be accused of being a foreign usurper. *Only* a black candidate with a foreign name would be accused of "palling around with domestic terrorists."

In the final analysis, when you boil away all of the weirdness, it becomes clear that the teabaggers are pissed because there isn't yet another doddering old white guy in the White House—*like they're used to*. That's what this is all about.

By way of a postscript, one of the many faceless radio talk show wing nuts, Jim Quinn, this week called President Obama a "Kenyan wuss" who should be "slapped silly." The Kenyan lie and the "slap silly" insult aside, this president is no wuss. You know how I know? He's a black man who ran for president and won despite the growing mob of gun-toting militant white bigots like Jim Quinn who are sucking air in America. President Obama achieving this despite the hatred and threats against him takes serious guts. Guts that Jim Quinn and the Tea Party movement will never understand.

The Tea Party Is Not a Haven for Racists

Cathy Young

Cathy Young writes a weekly column for Real Clear Politics, an independent political website. She is also a contributing editor at Reason *magazine.*

Ever since the "Tea Parties" gained national attention, the debate has raged on whether they are a grassroots protest movement in the proud tradition of American dissent, or a hysterical mob driven by fear, intolerance and selfishness. Recently, two much-discussed surveys—a CBS/*New York Times* poll and a multistate University of Washington poll—have been bandied about as proof that the leftist caricatures of the Tea Partiers as mean-spirited, rich, white bigots are accurate. Yet a look at the data suggests that this interpretation is highly skewed by political bias.

Tea Party Racial Views Reflect Mainstream Attitudes

In a Salon.com article titled "The Tea Partiers' Racial Paranoia," editor Joan Walsh notes that in the University of Washington [UW] poll, only 35% of pro–Tea Party whites regarded blacks as "hardworking," 45% as "intelligent," and 41% as "trustworthy." Walsh scoffs, "And Tea Party supporters don't like it when anyone notices the racists in their midst?"

Not so fast. The respondents in the UW poll were asked to rate on a 1–7 scale how intelligent, hardworking, and trustworthy they perceived "almost all" blacks (and, in separate questions, whites, Latinos, and Asians) to be. Whether the findings expose Tea Party bigotry hinges on two things: how

Cathy Young, "Tea Partiers Racist? Not So Fast," Real Clear Politics, April 25, 2010. www.realclearpolitics.com. Copyright © 2010 by Cathy Young. All rights reserved. Reproduced by permission of the author.

the "Tea Partiers'" opinions of blacks compare to their views of other groups, and how their answers compare to those of other, non-Tea-Partying Americans.

The UW researchers' initial analysis compared only whites who were strongly pro–Tea Party and strongly anti–Tea Party, concluding that the latter held a much more positive view of blacks. These data are no longer on the UW website; instead, there are tables for other race-related questions (such as "Over the past few years blacks have gotten less than they deserve"), with separate results for whites who were either neutral toward the Tea Party movement or had never heard of it, as well as for all whites.

But what about the racial stereotyping items? The lead investigator, political science professor Christopher Parker, graciously provided me with the fuller data—which strongly contradict the notion of the Tea Parties as a unique hotbed of racism.

The endurance of racial stereotypes in this day and age is disturbing; but Tea Party supporters differ little in this regard from mainstream Americans.

Thus, while only 35% of strong Tea Party supporters rated blacks as hardworking, only 49% described whites as such. While the gap is evident, these responses are close to those for all whites (blacks are rated as "hardworking" by 40%, whites by 52%). While whites who are strongly anti–Tea Party seem free of bias on this item—blacks and whites are rated as "hardworking" by 55% and 56%, respectively—this is not true for intelligence and trustworthiness. Whites in every group are less likely to rate blacks than whites as "intelligent" by similar margins: 14 points for Tea Party supporters (45% vs. 59%), 13 points for all whites (49% vs. 62%), 10 points for Tea Party opponents (59% vs. 69%). On "trustworthy," the gap is smaller in the pro–Tea Party group (41% vs. 49%) than in the anti–

Tea Party group (57% vs. 72%). One could write headlines about the "racial paranoia" of white liberals who consider blacks less trustworthy than whites!

The endurance of racial stereotypes in this day and age is disturbing; but Tea Party supporters differ little in this regard from mainstream Americans. (It is also worth noting that, as in many other surveys, Asian-Americans in the UW poll are rated much more positively than whites.)

Compared to middle-of-the-road whites, Tea Party supporters show far more agreement with the statement that blacks should work their way up "without special favors" the way other minorities such as Italians and Jews did, or that blacks would be as well-off as whites if they worked harder. The standard left-of-center view, shared by the UW researchers, is that such attitudes represent a subtler form of racism, or "racial resentment." In some cases, that is surely true. Yet these sentiments may also reflect a genuinely race-neutral belief in self-reliance and self-help—or the view, shared by many black commentators, that the black community's problems are partly rooted in damaging behavioral and cultural patterns.

John McWhorter, a noted black scholar and author whose works include the 2000 book, *Losing the Race: Self-Sabotage in Black America*, says that "the idea that 'racism' is behind the Tea Partiers is based on a lazy and vain extension of the term 'racism' to meaning 'that which many black people would not approve of.'" According to McWhorter, "The position that the government does too much to help black people is not necessarily one based in inherent bias against people with black skin—it can be argued as a reasonable proposition based on the spotty record of social programs since the 1960s."

The other charge against Tea Partiers is that they are not "the people" but the privileged defending their privilege. Walsh gleefully points out that in the *Times*/CBS poll, 12% of Tea Party sympathizers had an annual income over $250,000—forgetting to mention that so did 11% of all Americans. *Wash-*

ington Post columnist E.J. Dionne asserts that "Tea Party enthusiasts ... side with the better-off against the poor": 73% of them, versus 38% of all Americans, say that "providing government benefits to poor people encourages them to remain poor." (Of course, they couldn't possibly be sincere in the belief that poor people are often harmed more than helped by government programs.)

> *The Tea Partiers are disproportionately Republican and right-wing.*

A Conservative Movement

What, then, do the new polls tell us about the Tea Partiers—or, at least, Tea Party sympathizers? (In the *Times*/CBS poll, only one in five self-identified Tea Party supporters reported actual involvement in Tea Party activities.) They are mostly white and more likely to be male (59%); three-quarters are 45 and older, compared to half of all Americans. They are more religious than average, though not dramatically so: 39% are evangelical Christians and 38% attend church every week, while the figures for all Americans are 28% and 27%.

Not surprisingly, the Tea Partiers are disproportionately Republican and right-wing: 39% consider themselves "very conservative" and 34% "somewhat conservative" (compared to 12% and 24%, respectively, of the general population). Their conservatism, moreover, tends to be more authoritarian than libertarian: In the UW poll, pro–Tea Party respondents are much more likely than others to agree that the government should be able to detain suspects indefinitely without trial and to tap phones if there is a threat of terrorism.

In other words, the Tea Party movement is mainly conservative—which is hardly the stuff of headlines. That does not make it a haven for racists.

While the Tea Partiers raise important questions about the growth of government, they certainly have their darker side:

too often, they promote the politics of personal attack and demonization, of hyperbole and hysteria (though they are no more guilty of this than were [George W.] Bush-era protesters on the left). Yet to respond with more hyperbole, demonization and hysteria directed at the Tea Partiers themselves will not address the problems but only compound the damage.

Race Is Not the Motivator Behind Tea Party Activism

Robert Chapman-Smith

Robert Chapman-Smith is a Republican politician who has served in both the US House of Representatives and the Senate.

I ask myself what's so different about [President Barack] Obama, and the answer is pretty obvious: He's black.—Eugene Robinson

Washington Post columnist and Pulitzer Prize–winning journalist Eugene Robinson is befuddled by the rise of conservatism in the Age of Obama. Mr. Robinson is not alone in his bewilderment. Most of the media, and especially the left-leaning media, find the Tea Party to be an enigma wrapped in a paradox. The media's confusion is wrought from the myriad of messages streaming from multiple Tea Party factions. But it is one thing to be puzzled by a decentralized political movement and quite another thing to be *entirely ignorant of blatant historical facts.*

Mr. Robinson starts his column by pulling the "I'm not calling you a racist, but you're a racist" line. It's simply mind-numbing that people who comment on the Tea Party fail to recognize the disingenuous nature of claiming race as a motivating factor while simultaneously claiming that a person supremely motivated by race is not a racist.

Lazy Arguments

Mr. Robinson then engages the tired meme that the Tea Party's "take our country back" rhetoric is coded language motivated by the president's darkened hue. If Mr. Robinson had cared to venture past his *a priori* [predetermined, not based on facts]

Robert Chapman-Smith, "Roots of Tea Party Rage," *American Conservative*, November 2, 2010. Copyright © 2010 by Robert Chapman-Smith. All rights reserved. Reproduced by permission of American Conservative LLC.

armchair reasoning, he might have discovered that former DNC [Democratic National Committee] Chairman Howard Dean published a book with the ominous title: *You Have the Power: How to Take Back Our Country and Restore Democracy in America*. Like most bumper slogan phrases, "take back our country" is innocuous and largely empty rhetoric used to stoke the fires of the political base. If Tea Party politicians succeed in gaining offices and implementing policy that is diametrically opposed to progressive ideology, then look for the left to start reusing an iteration of the "take our country back" meme.

Mr. Robinson proceeds from here to ponder why the Tea Party did not stir under George W. Bush's presidency. Mr. Robinson is correct that it was our 43rd president who signed the monstrous Wall Street bailout, who launched two wars, and who added to our entitlement burden by greatly expanding Medicare. But Mr. Robinson is wrong in thinking that the Tea Party is not a product of George W. Bush's legacy. Without President Bush's tenure in office, Ron Paul would not have had a quarter of the momentum he had in the 2008 presidential campaign. Ron Paul held the first Tea Party protest on December 16, 2007—before Barack Obama was even a twinkle in [political commentator] Chris Matthews's eye. Ron Paul's antigovernment campaign message resonated on a Republican platform that lived through eight years of big spending compassionate conservatism. Ron Paul's campaign consciously invoked the imagery of the original 1773 Boston Tea Party. On Tax Day 2008, thousands took part in protests aimed at spreading the anti–big government and low-tax message. At this point in the campaign, Senator Obama was the clear front-runner, but it'd be beyond a stretch to say the backlash against government was engendered by Mr. Obama's eventual nomination. Rather, the roots of the Tea Party are precisely what Mr. Robinson thinks they are not: a repudiation of President Bush's terms in office.

So why is the message so acute now? Perhaps part of the vitriol stems from the fact that Presidents Bush and Obama differ in name, but not in policy. Perhaps the partisan attitudes that suppressed backlash against President Bush from the right do not act as restraints for criticism of Obama. (Notice how politicians like Madam [former Speaker of the House Nancy] Pelosi and groups like Project Pink, some of the loudest voices against the use of force abroad, haven't uttered so much as a peep against Obama for continuing and extending horrific Bush-era foreign policy doctrines.) Perhaps it is due to the fact that our post-partisan president is anything but post-partisan. Perhaps it is because President Obama promised change and in return for his election America has received, as Reason TV illustrates, more of the same. And let us not forget that the coordinating powers of the Internet had yet to be fully utilized by politicians and grassroots under President Bush's reign. So perhaps the reason the voice of the Tea Party is so much louder is due to conservatives mirroring Ron Paul and Barack Obama's brilliant Internet campaigns.

Like most bumper slogan phrases, "take back our country" is innocuous and largely empty rhetoric used to stoke the fires of the political base.

There is no denying that race plays a role in the American psyche, but to ignore obvious facts of history in favor of a media narrative that race is the *primary* motivating factor behind the Tea Party is intellectually lazy.

African American Tea Party Activists See No Racism in the Movement

Aaron Goldstein

Aaron Goldstein is a Canadian-born writer and political commentator, as well as a frequent contributor to conservative publications.

Is calling Tea Party activists racist the best liberals can do?

Consider the thoughts of the inaptly named openmind82 in a post titled "Is the Tea Party or Conservs [Conservatives] the Modern Day Klan?" on the *Daily Kos*:

> When I hear words yelled like, "Faggot, N-----" or politicians being cursed and spit on, then one has to believe it's no longer about politics, but about something else. And it's RACISM, it's always been about racism, you know it, I know it, and the media knows or at least they pretend not to.
>
> These people can't stand to see people of color, gays, and women making legislative decisions that can effect (sic) our country. It's about a fringe group of racist conservatives and libertarians using anti-government rhetoric to hide their racist feelings, and this health reform simply exposed them.

Then there are those who simply object to Tea Party activists being melatonin challenged. Frank Rich of the *New York Times* writes, "The Tea Party movement is virtually all white." Charles Blow, Rich's colleague at the *Times*, elaborated on this thought by describing a poll about Tea Party activists by Quinnipiac University. Blow states the poll "found them to be just

Aaron Goldstein, "The Color of Tea," *American Spectator*, April 8, 2010. Copyright © 2010 by Aaron Goldstein. All rights reserved. Reproduced by permission of The American Spectator.

as anachronistic to the direction of the country's demographics as the Republican Party. For instance, they were disproportionately white, evangelical Christian and 'less educated ... than the average Joe and Jane Six-Pack.'"

Black Tea Party Activists See No Racism

Well, so much for living in a country where people are judged by the content of their character. When in the company of Tea Party activists, Kevin Jackson, Pastor C.L. Bryant, and Deneen Borelli are judged not only by the content of their character but by the content of their message. They are Tea Party activists who happen to be black. Recently, I spoke with each of them over the phone.

Between them they have addressed over one hundred Tea Party rallies in the past year. If the Tea Party is as "comedienne" Janeane Garofalo claims nothing more than "racism straight up" then one would think that Jackson, Bryant, and Borelli would be at risk of imminent harm and infectious hatred. But the only infectious quality these three have encountered amongst Tea Party activists is their enthusiasm.

Of course, it doesn't stop Colbert King of the *Washington Post* or Rep. James Clyburn from comparing Tea Party activists to segregationists in the South. Yet I don't seem to recall segregationists in the South inviting black speakers to address their rallies.

> "[The Tea Party activists] care about your character, not your color."

Kevin Jackson, author of the book *The Big Black Lie: [How I Learned the Truth About the Democrat Party]*, told me unequivocally that the allegations of racism leveled against Tea Party activists last month [March 2010] by Rep. John Lewis and other members of the Congressional Black Caucus are "complete fabrications" and feelings of racism amongst Tea

Party activists "don't exist." Of course, that doesn't deter Lewis and company. Jackson states, "It's their number one weapon to try to discredit the Tea Party." While Jackson said he would like to see more involvement in the Tea Party amongst blacks (especially black youth), he does not feel out of place in the least. "No racism has been done to me," said Jackson.

In fact, Jackson went on to say the only thing that would stir violence amongst fellow Tea Party activists would be towards displays of racist behavior. Thus the allegations leveled by Lewis and others are incongruent with his experience. Not only does Jackson find that his Tea Party speeches regularly receive standing ovations but he also finds himself invited out to dinner, to go fishing and asked "to marry their daughters." If that doesn't tell you racism is clinically dead in this country, then nothing will. "They care about your character, not your color," Jackson said.

"The Tea Party's message of small government and self-reliance is resonating with people and the liberal/left doesn't want that message to get out."

Pastor Bryant became a Tea Party activist completely by accident. Although Bryant describes himself as "an independent, fiscal conservative," he had no illusions of becoming a political activist. However, when Bryant and his wife showed up early at a Tea Party rally in Bossier City, Louisiana, and decided to help the organizers set up, he made quite the impression. As the minister presiding over the Cedar Hills Baptist Church in the village of Grand Cane near Shreveport, Bryant is quite accustomed to speaking before large crowds. They would not regret their decision to add Bryant to their roster of speakers.

Before long Bryant would be speaking all over the country spreading the gospel of liberty. Bryant, a New Orleans Saints fan, would even be well received by Indianapolis Colts fans in

Hoosier country. Bryant's reputation as an orator is such that he has been invited to introduce both Glenn Beck [conservative radio and television host] and Sarah Palin [the former governor of Alaska and 2008 vice presidential candidate] at upcoming Tea Party rallies. He also hosts a radio program called *Hot Tea Radio*.

Bryant told me the motivations of Tea Party activists have "nothing to do with a black president" and that accusations of racism are little more than "an intentional smear campaign against regular Americans." "It's not a black thing. It's not a white thing. We are fiscal conservatives who don't feel we are being represented," said Bryant.

Deneen Borelli, a fellow with the black conservative network and policy think tank Project 21, has a different take on the charges of racism against the Tea Party. Borelli, who specializes in energy policy and is a contributor to the Fox News Channel, told me such allegations are indications that the Tea Party is "making a difference." She elaborated by stating, "The Tea Party's message of small government and self-reliance is resonating with people and the liberal/left doesn't want that message to get out." Borelli dismisses allegations of racism as little more than "a tactic to stifle debate."

If left-wing politicians and the liberal media persist in calling Tea Party activists racist, then it is up to Americans of all colors to tell them they have to do better.

Claims of Racism in the Tea Party Are Hyperbole

Michael C. Moynihan

Michael C. Moynihan is a senior editor of Reason, *a libertarian magazine.*

On November 9, 1938, in the Tyrolian city of Innsbruck, Richard Berger, president of the local Jewish community, was snatched from his home and beaten to death with rocks and rifle butts, his body deposited in a nearby river. On the same evening, in an apartment building on Gänsbacherstrasse, Karl Bauer, of whom little is known besides his religious affiliation and his activities on behalf of Innsbruck's Jewish community, was beaten to death by plainclothes members of the SS [a paramilitary group under Nazi control]. The vulturine horde moved swiftly upstairs, where they found the *Volksfeind* Richard Graubart, also Jewish. He was stabbed to death as his wife and daughter looked on.

This is a small window into the wanton brutality that was *Reichskristallnacht*—often called the "Night of Broken Glass"—in a medium-sized Austrian city. A contemporaneous report compiled in Berlin and presided over by the gruesome SS butcher Reinhard Heydrich estimated that 36 Jews were killed across the German *Reich*. It was, as historian Saul Friedländer has observed, a rather conservative guess: "Apart from the 267 synagogues destroyed and the 7,500 businesses vandalized, some ninety-one Jews had been killed all over Germany and hundreds more had committed suicide or died as a result of mistreatment in the camps."

Would you be surprised to learn that a similar spasm of violence was recently visited upon African American politi-

Michael C. Moynihan, "Red America, White Power. Is the Tea Party Movement Motivated by Race Hatred?" *Reason* magazine and Reason.com, April 1, 2010. www.reason.com. Copyright © 2010 by Michael C. Moynihan. All rights reserved. Reproduced by permission of Reason Foundation.

Is the Tea Party Movement Racist?

cians in Washington, D.C.? Well, credulous reader, the *New York Times* recently told us that the shock troops of the Tea Party movement engaged in a "small-scale mimicry of *Kristallnacht*" while protesting the passage of a treasury-busting health care bill.

No Mass Genocide at Tea Party Rally

This bizarre invocation of genocide was to be found on the op-ed page, from the hysterical ex-theater critic and Tea Party obsessive [columnist] Frank Rich. Whether or not Rich is aware of it—and when one ascends to the position of *New York Times* columnist, ignorance is an unconvincing excuse—it is to mass killings that the reader's mind wanders when the 20th century's most famous pogrom is invoked. In a book of essays analyzing the events of 1938, the scholar Walter H. Pehle's chosen title lays down the marker: *[November 1938:] From 'Kristallnacht' to Genocide*. The anti-Semitic attacks, "spontaneously" carried out "in reaction" to the murder of a Nazi diplomat, were the beginnings of a program of systematic genocide. Surely Rich, a professional writer his entire adult life, understands that the English language is abundant enough to allow for nuance and precision.

No one was stabbed this March [2010 at the Tea Party march on Washington], no limp bodies dumped into the Anacostia River, no buildings burned. A few lunkheads broke windows ... and one unidentified protester called Rep. Barney Frank (D-Mass.) a "faggot," for which he was rebuked by fellow protesters. Despite gleeful recitation by the media, claims of racial taunts directed at African-American congressmen have yet to be substantiated—but more on that in a moment.

Eliminationist Rhetoric

One stray columnist comparing the rowdy Tea Party crowds to German *genocidaires* could perhaps be explained away. An inattentive editor, a moment of regretful anger seeping into the prose. But to Rich's colleague Paul Krugman, the hyperpartisan economist and Nobel Prize winner, the Nazi comparison was a useful one, although it did demand subtlety. "What has been really striking," Krugman wrote after the health care bill passed, "has been the *eliminationist rhetoric* of the G.O.P. [the Republican Party], coming not from some radical fringe but from the party's leaders" (emphasis added).

If your dictionary is unfamiliar with the word *eliminationist*, that's because of the term's recent vintage, coined in 1996 by Harvard political scientist Daniel Jonah Goldhagen. In his book *Hitler's Willing Executioners: Ordinary Germans and the Holocaust*, Goldhagen argued that far from being bullied and terrorized into allowing its government to commit genocide in their name, most Germans were imbued with an *eliminationist* hatred of Jews—i.e., a desire that Jews be eliminated from Aryan society—which transitioned smoothly into an *exterminationist* orgy of violence.

Of the 40 references to "eliminationism" in the *Times* archive, all but one refer to the destruction of European Jewry. The sole standout is Krugman, who, as we have seen, is referencing the Republican Party's opposition to health care legislation....

Other Examples of Hyperbole

Moving down market to the *New York Daily News*, one finds a column by sports columnist Mike Lupica declaring that the crowds of health care protesters are "no longer about political dissent. It is about storm trooper sound bites, and hate." It is unclear what a "storm trooper sound bite" is (or why this would be incompatible with "political dissent," no matter how noxious), though Lupica is unambiguously guiding readers towards the Nazi image; towards the brown-shirted tough rounding up dissidents, cracking jaws, and kicking teeth.

Examining the Tea Party protesters, *Washington Post* columnist Colbert King saw faces whose very visual cues betrayed direct lineage to overt racists from a half century before. "Those same jeering faces," King wrote, "could be seen gathered around the Arkansas National Guard troopers who blocked nine black children from entering Little Rock's Central High School in 1957." If the examples of Alabama and Mississippi in the 1950s were too distant, King told readers that he had also seen those very faces in the 1990s, at a rally in support of neo-Nazi agitator David Duke.

It is depressing that, for quick political gain, people like King will debase the legacy of the civil rights movement by comparing peaceful (and often misguided) protesters with the thuggery of Bull Connor and the racist Birmingham police department. But just when it looked like we had scraped the bottom of the hyperbole barrel, the always vapid Jesse Jackson told the breast-obsessed readers of the *Huffington Post* that the Tea Partiers reminded him of an era when some Americans responded to social change "with terror, bombed churches, and killed freedom marchers."

Many referenced the claim that Rep. John Lewis (D-Ga.) was, in Rep. Emanuel Cleaver (D-Mo.) description, met with a "chorus," of racist taunts, though no evidence has materialized to substantiate these accusations—and the alleged chorus occurred in an area with a higher video camera density than a Paris Hilton birthday party. Indeed, claims that Cleaver was spat upon were debunked when video surfaced of a spittle-flecked protester who shouted "kill the bill" as the congressman passed, but not deliberately hocking a loogie on him.

It isn't unreasonable to think that amongst the Tea Party protesters one can find the ignorant and hateful.

No Proof of Racist Motivations

So if the events on Capitol Hill were indeed the moral equivalent of a "mini-Kristallnacht," then questioning this tale of racism is a [Holocaust denier] David Irving-like act, right?

Those who wondered about the contradicting claims surrounding the Lewis charge were, naturally, themselves derided as racist. But if the country's largest newspapers can accuse those assembled to "kill the bill" of being motivated by racial animus, "eliminationism," Nazism, or old Dixie nostalgia, is it so unfair to ask for verifiable proof?

It isn't unreasonable to think that amongst the Tea Party protesters one can find the ignorant and hateful. Many of the protesters seem to believe that the president of the United States of America is a Communist, demonstrating that they have a level of historical understanding on par with Frank Rich. But that critique is something rather different than imputing a racist motivation to anyone deeply concerned about an enormously expensive health care bill.

Some of this is the problem of *now*, of rendering apocalyptic judgments about events that are only just unfolding. In the weeks following the 9/11 attacks [September 11, 2001, terrorist attacks on the United States], *Vanity Fair* editor Graydon Carter declared solemnly and with regret that irony had vanished in the smoke and embers of the demolished World Trade Center, a judgment that seemed plausible at the time. Rereading some of the commentary produced in the aftermath of the attacks is like looking at old high school yearbook photos—good god, what *were* we thinking? Likewise, a journalist who chased [former president] Bill Clinton scandals for a conservative magazine in the 1990s recently told me how silly it all seemed with the clarifying benefit of hindsight. At the time, he said, it all seemed so reasonable.

And while we are on the topic of 9/11, how quickly we forget that in the editorial rooms and barrooms of the [George W.] Bush era, the vapid phrase on the lips of my liberal-minded comrades, repeated like a Maharishi mantra, was that "dissent is patriotic." Now dissent has become the first indication of incipient fascism and subterranean racism. If Rich sees in the current debate the seeds of pogrom, if Krugman sees the rhetoric of "eliminationism," forget national health care—we need a national history lesson.

CHAPTER 3

Is the Tea Party Movement Compatible with the Republican Party?

Chapter Preface

Rand Paul, a forty-seven-year-old ophthalmologist from Bowling Green, Kentucky, and son of well-known libertarian congressman Ron Paul (a Republican from Texas), won a US Senate seat on November 3, 2010, by decisively defeating his Democratic opponent. Paul ran as a Tea Party candidate, and in his election night victory speech, he announced: "I have a message from the Tea Party. A message that is loud and clear and does not mince words: We have come to take our government back."[1] Many commentators say that Rand Paul's election to the Senate makes him the default leader of the Tea Party.

As a candidate, Rand Paul ran on many of the broad themes embraced by Tea Party supporters, including cutting federal spending, reducing taxes, and balancing the federal budget. However, as a libertarian long schooled by his father, Rand Paul also included some familiar libertarian ideas. Libertarians, for example, believe that individual rights should be maximized and that government powers should be sharply curtailed; therefore, one of Rand Paul's goals is to curb the clout of the Federal Reserve (the Fed), the nation's central bank and controller of the US money supply. Both Ron and Rand Paul view the Fed's ability to create money without accountability to Congress as a secret tax on Americans and a prime example of too much government power. In addition, Rand Paul railed against the federal government's decision to bail out big banks, and he has promised to slash federal agencies like the Department of Education, ban earmarks, and introduce congressional term limits.

Now that Rand Paul is part of the US Senate, the question is what impact he and fellow Tea Party supporters will have

---

1. Quoted in Alex Altman, "Rand Paul's Tea Party Triumph in Kentucky," *Time*, May 19, 2010. www.time.com.

on the Republican Party and on future legislation. Some reports identify up to five new Republican senators and up to twenty new Republican representatives as Tea Party supporters. One line of thinking is that these Tea Party activists will be such a small minority within the Republican Party that they will either be completely ineffective at pushing their agenda among establishment Republicans or that they will be reduced to a vocal voice for core Republican voters and enjoy only symbolic victories. One example of the latter is a vote on repealing the health care legislation that was supported by President Barack Obama and passed by Congress in 2010. Such a vote did take place on January 19, 2011, and did pass in the Republican-controlled House, but it was defeated on February 2, 2011, in the Democrat-controlled Senate. In addition, many analysts have predicted that the Tea Party unity will be threatened by differing views on a number of social and foreign policy issues. Although generally in agreement about budget and fiscal responsibility issues, for example, some Tea Party supporters as well as many establishment Republicans may not agree with pro-libertarian ideas such as Rand Paul's opposition to the war in Iraq and his distaste for massive military spending.

Other political commentators, however, think that Rand Paul and his Tea Party colleagues could have more political clout than many people think. Paul has suggested creating a bicameral Tea Party caucus composed of both senators and representatives, to try to shape the national debate on fiscal and other issues in coming years. Such a group might be linked to grassroots Tea Party organizations and could be a way for the Tea Party to garner press attention and promote its agenda within the Congress. Other commentators predict that Rand Paul could follow in the footsteps of his father who is called Dr. No because of his repeated votes against almost every spending or tax bill introduced in the House of Representatives. Political experts say that Ron Paul's no votes in the

House have had mostly symbolic effect, but in the Senate, which is so much smaller than the House, a single opposition vote or a few votes could be used in various parliamentary ways to effectively block legislation. If Rand Paul and other Senate Tea Party supporters follow this path, they could potentially create enormous leverage by threatening to derail various types of spending bills, including many that are necessary to fund critical programs and keep the federal government from defaulting on its obligations.

In time, the public will have a better idea of how the Tea Party will impact the Republican Party and the work of Congress. Rand Paul's book, *The Tea Party Goes to Washington*, reveals a plan for implementing Tea Party goals in the Senate. The authors of the viewpoints in this chapter provide a range of views about the Tea Party's compatibility with the Republican Party and the viability of Tea Party policy views.

Tea Party Activists Are Just Republicans by Another Name

Perrspectives

Perrspectives is a website dedicated to examining politics, culture, and society.

As a quick look back at any McCain-Palin rally [referring to the Republican ticket of Senator John McCain and Sarah Palin in the 2008 presidential race] in the fall of 2008 will confirm, the Tea Party movement hardly began with the inauguration of Barack Obama. But for all intents and purposes, it ended yesterday [November 2, 2010]. As it turns out, the Tea Party's looming demise stems not from its failure at the polls, but from its now largely successful transformation of the GOP [the Republican Party].

Not, of course, according to the media reaction to Tuesday's red midterm tsunami. Pointing to easy wins by Tea Party favorites Rand Paul and Marco Rubio, the *New York Times* announced, "Victories Suggest Wider Appeal of Tea Party." While CNN declared, "Election Projections Fuel Tea Party Fervor," the *Wall Street Journal* proclaimed, "Tea Party Plan for Next Phase."

But largely lost in that seeming consensus about the triumph of right-wing populist anger is the inescapable truth about the Tea Partiers. That is, these older, whiter and more ideologically conservative voters are just Republicans by another name. And by the time the 2012 GOP presidential primaries roll around, they will be indistinguishable from the rest of the Republican hard-line base.

Jon Perr, "The End of the Tea Party," Perrspectives, November 3, 2010. (http://www.perrspectives.com/blog/archives/002013.htm). Copyright © 2010 by Jon Perr. All rights reserved. Reproduced by permission of the author. Perrspectives can be found online at www.perrspectives.com.

Voting like Republicans

To be sure, the 2010 exit polls confirmed that Tea Party members are just Republicans who shout louder. The national House exit poll found that 40 percent of those surveyed supported the Tea Party. That's virtually identical to the 41 percent favorable opinion of the Republican Party. Unsurprisingly, their behavior in the voting booth was also indistinguishable, as the GOP captured 87 percent of the Tea Party members' ballots.

Which is precisely what months of polling suggested. In March, a Quinnipiac University poll found that 74 percent are Republicans or independent voters leaning Republican while 77 percent voted for Sen. John McCain in 2008. Those findings echo a February CNN survey which similarly demolished the myth of the Tea Bagger-as-independent. As CNN polling director Keating Holland noted:

> "87 percent say they would vote for the GOP candidate in their congressional district if there were no third-party candidate endorsed by the Tea Party."

Looking like Republicans

And they just don't vote like Republicans; they look like them, too.

Tea Party members are just Republicans who shout louder.

Earlier this year, Gallup and Winston Group like Quinnipiac and CNN before them confirmed that the vast majority of Tea Party members are ideologically conservative and consistently vote Republican. As Gallup concluded:

> "Tea Party supporters are decidedly Republican and conservative in their leanings. Also, compared with average Americans, supporters are slightly more likely to be male and less likely to be lower-income."

And very white. While 63 percent of white men and 58 percent of white women voted Republican in Tuesday's House races, Tea Partiers were no doubt well represented in their ranks. (Their presence is also reflected by the GOP's embrace of the Tea Party's Birther, Deather, Obama-as-Muslim and other myths [references to false beliefs that Obama was not born in the United States, that health care reform would result in the deaths of senior citizens, and that Obama is a Muslim].) Of the 8 percent of those claiming illegal immigration was the most important issue facing the nation, a whopping 69 percent backed the GOP. Again, as a University of Washington study suggested in April 2010, the Tea Party faithful were doubtless among them in large numbers:

> Approximately 45% of whites either strongly or somewhat approve of the movement. Of those, only 35% believe blacks to be hardworking, only 45% believe blacks are intelligent, and only 41% think that blacks are trustworthy. Perceptions of Latinos aren't much different. While 50% of white Tea Party supporters believe Latinos to be hardworking, only 39% think them intelligent, and at 37%, fewer Tea Party supporters believe Latinos to be trustworthy.

The Tea Party members' policy prescriptions are pretty much the same toxic brew cooked up by the Republican leadership.

Republican Policies

Despite their much-publicized purge of party moderates, the Tea Baggers' policy prescriptions are pretty much the same toxic brew cooked up by the Republican leadership. The Tea Party "Contract from America" and the GOP "Pledge to America" are almost carbon copies. Both call for the repeal of health care reform and opposition to cap-and-trade energy legislation. Both support making the budget-busting Bush tax cuts permanent, including the repeal of the estate tax and another $700 billion windfall for the wealthiest 2 percent of Americans. While only the GOP pledge did not echo the Tea Party call for a balanced budget amendment to the Constitution, Republican stars from Tim Pawlenty and Lindsey Graham to Marco Rubio and Rand Paul did. (Of course, while Tea Party members and Republicans alike demand deep federal spending cuts, neither will state what those cuts might be.)

And the GOP is not only reading from the same playbook as the Tea Partiers, its new leadership long ago welcomed its players with open arms. South Carolina Senator Jim DeMint, who today authored a *Wall Street Journal* op-ed telling them to "Put on your boxing gloves.... The fight begins today," said last December:

> "We need to stop looking at the tea parties as separate from the Republican Party. If we do that, we can stand up and create the biggest tent of all."

In the House, Tea Party caucus chair Michele Bachmann announced her intent to land the number three slot in the Republican leadership. But months ago, she explained her strategy for Republican renewal:

> "Well, it's embraced the Tea Party movement with full arms ... if the Republican Party is wise, they will allow themselves to be re-defined by the Tea Party movement. And I hope that that will be the case."

Indeed, it now is. As the *Wall Street Journal* reported:

> Ms. [Tea Party leader Jenny Beth] Martin said Tea Party Patriots is finalizing plans for a summit and "orientation" Nov. 14 in Washington for all freshman members of Congress. Newly elected officials will meet "face to face" with 200 or more local Tea Party coordinators from around the country, she said. Her group is working on a legislative agenda to

present then. The focus: Balance the federal budget; and repeal "100 percent repeal" of the health care overhaul.

"We're going to talk to them about what we expect from them," she said, "and what they can expect from us if they don't uphold our core values."

Jenny Beth Martin need not worry. She had them at hello. And vice versa.

Any Republican White House hopeful heading to Iowa to kick-start the 2012 campaign ignores that at his or her peril. The hard-liners who in 2008 chose Mike Huckabee while citing immigration as their number one issue during a time of economic crisis are waiting.

Back in April 2009, the *Daily Show*'s Jon Stewart offered some sound advice for frothing at the mouth Tea Party members, "I think you might be confusing tyranny with losing." Now that Republicans are winning again, they won't have nearly so much to be angry about.

The Tea Party Is Just More Republican Radicalism

Tim Rutten

Tim Rutten is a journalist who writes for the Los Angeles Times, *a daily US newspaper.*

In an afterword appended to the White House diaries he published this week [September 20, 2010], former president [Jimmy] Carter muses, "It may be difficult for some younger readers to realize how much the Washington political scene has changed in the last 30 years."

Carter points out that the congressional bipartisanship on which he relied for his considerable number of legislative achievements no longer exists and that the "pernicious effects of partisanship have not been limited to Washington; American citizens have also become more polarized in their beliefs. . . . Almost all segments of American society—the poor, the middle class and the wealthy—have become more alienated from our government. Observing the behavior of the Washington political establishment, people too often feel only frustration and mistrust; inevitably, we now see frequent exhibitions of anger and vituperation."

It's impossible to quarrel with Carter's characterization, and equally impossible not to notice that in an era when people speak only to those who share their particular angry haze, the politics of delusion and self-deception flourish. Take the current midterm election campaign, in which it has become commonplace for Republican/"Tea" Party candidates—the two names now are interchangeable—to assail President [Barack] Obama's alleged radicalism and his purported plan to transform the United States into a European-style social democracy.

Tim Rutten, "The GOP/'Tea' Party Radicalism," *Los Angeles Times*, September 22, 2010. Copyright © 2010. All rights reserved. Reproduced by permission.

Putting aside the nonsensical nature of these claims, what's startling is the unchallenged way in which they rhetorically invert the factual geography of the electoral landscape. In fact, it's been more than a century since a viable party has nominated as many candidates with such radical views for federal office as the Republican/Tea Party has this year.

The Tea Party Is Republican Radicalism

Writing in Tuesday's [September 21, 2010] *Wall Street Journal*, Mississippi Gov. Haley Barbour, chairman of the Republican Governors Assn., said that electorally speaking, you now can "replace 'Tea Party' with 'Republican' . . . and each description would remain totally accurate." The voters who support the GOP [Republican] Tea Party, he wrote, "fear that their children and grandchildren won't inherit the same country they inherited from their parents and grandparents."

The irony here is that electing the candidates Barbour hails will guarantee that the children will inherit a country their great-grandparents overwhelmingly rejected—one that existed in Herbert Hoover's era or, in some cases, before the Civil War. In fact, none of the five Republican presidents who've held office since the [Great] Depression have advanced anything like the current GOP/Tea Party's radical agenda.

> *It's been more than a century since a viable party has nominated as many candidates with such radical views for federal office as the Republican/Tea Party has [in 2010].*

It's hard to tell exactly what Christine O'Donnell, the Republican nominee for a Senate seat in Delaware, believes, though we do know that she's dabbled in witchcraft, doesn't pay her bills and thinks scientists are breeding mice with human brains. In Kentucky, senatorial candidate Rand Paul wants to eliminate the Departments of Education and Energy, as does Alaskan nominee Joe Miller, who also says that unemployment insurance is unconstitutional. In Utah, GOP Senate hopeful Mike Lee wants to repeal or amend the 14th and 17th Amendments, thereby doing away with our current citizenship laws and the popular election of U.S. senators. [Senate candidate] Sharron Angle in Nevada has ruminated about abolishing both Social Security and Medicare.

There's actually less difference than one might think between the views of these Tea Party "insurgents" and those of establishment Republicans. If, as now seems possible, the Republicans recapture the House, two incumbent congressmen with an outsized say on budgetary policies will be Wisconsin's Paul D. Ryan and Virginia's Eric Cantor. Both already have signed off on a plan to privatize Social Security and to replace Medicare with a vague voucher system. Meanwhile, former Republican House Majority Leader Dick Armey denounces Social Security as a fraud and a Ponzi scheme.

Sen. James M. Inhofe of Oklahoma, who would replace Barbara Boxer as chairman of the Committee on Environment and Public Works if the GOP recaptures the Senate, believes that global warming is "the greatest hoax ever perpetrated on the American people." Then there's presidential hopeful Newt Gingrich, who fulminated darkly about anti-Christian liberal plots and wants to pass laws banning the imposition of Sharia [Islamic] law. (We're all losing sleep over that prospect.)

There's actually less difference than one might think between the views of ... Tea Party "insurgents" and those of establishment Republicans.

Picture for a second an America without Social Security, Medicare or unemployment insurance. Imagine this country without the 14th or 17th Amendments or effective federal oversight of education or energy.

The rude beast of radicalism may be slouching toward the polls in November [2010], but it didn't start out from the White House.

The Tea Party Message Is an Ultraconservative Republican One

Ole Ole Olson

Ole Ole Olson is senior news editor and chief news media strategist for News Junkie Post, a web-based news site for relevant articles and videos on US and world affairs, politics, the environment, and entertainment.

For those who understand the nature of politics, the new Tea Party movement has always been extremely transparent. All of the frustration, anger, and disillusionment stemming from 30 years of failures stemming from conservative policies in every realm was manifesting itself in a mass awakening; a rejection of the messages coming from the levers of power both inside and outside the government was brewing.

This awakening manifested itself into the movement for change, a new progressive political paradigm that rejected the failed conservative dogma and tapped into this rage the public felt. Where conservative foreign policy had brought us massive lies to lead us into a war for oil, secret torture facilities, and some really sinister shit, the new progressive paradigm called for a reset of diplomatic solutions, humanitarian gestures, and shrinking the massive military machine.

Where conservative domestic policy had brought the country widespread domestic spying on the public, an administration that favored loyalty over competence, and a free hand to help multinational corporations exploit both the environment and working men and women, the new progressive paradigm

Ole Ole Olson, "A Progressive Response to Tea Party Contract from America," News Junkie Post, April 23, 2010. www.newsjunkiepost.com. Copyright © 2010 by Ole Ole Olson. All rights reserved. Reproduced by permission of the author.

called for protecting the poor and middle class, striving for transparency in government, and protecting our planet for our children's generation.

Where conservative economic policy brought about rampant deregulation, empowering greed for corporations, massive tax cuts and wealth consolidation for the rich, and the mother of all recessions, the new progressive paradigm called for opportunity for all Americans, strong regulations to ensure ethical practices, and creating jobs.

Corporate front groups like FreedomWorks and Americans for Prosperity [took] . . . over the fledgling grassroots libertarian movement known as the Tea Parties.

Harnessing Anger to Double Down on Conservative Policies

These are dangerous notions for the corporations and wealthy that have so consolidated their hold over the political process by controlling and dominating campaign contributions, so an idea was hatched. Corporate front groups like FreedomWorks and Americans for Prosperity would take over the fledgling grassroots libertarian movement known as the Tea Parties, which actually began as Ron Paul campaign events in 2007. After initially hiding behind the libertarian banner to avoid blame for the disastrous culmination of their conservative policies, they would then purge real libertarians from the ranks, and slowly shift the message to more of an ultraconservative, traditional Republican one.

We have seen this in action. Where the first messages were strictly about fiscal responsibility, now the plethora of messages are religious, anti-immigrant, anti-environment, and anti-health care reform. The libertarians who opposed torture, the Iraq War, domestic espionage, imposing one religion on all of society, and legalizing marijuana are no longer welcome at any rally.

Despite this transition, the overall scheme worked: *the anger and resentment against conservative policies had been shifted first to the government as a whole, and now to progressive Democrats who are trying to reform the system.* The deliberate obstructionism and blatant negative propaganda have convinced many that somehow the reformers are actually to blame for the mess our nation is in, and that they need to be punished at the polls in these November [2010] midterm elections.

I know, the Tea Party claims to be nonpartisan and their official stance is that "everyone" should be voted out in November, but in reality the movement has turned into the extreme ultraconservative side of the Republican Party, and the only Republicans they are actually targeting are the center-right ones who actually might compromise once in a while for the sake of the nation. The Tea Party now has one goal: to replace anyone not Far Right in the government. In this case, that usually means the Democrats.

The New Contract from America

Analysts have recognized this for a year. However, for the public, it has been difficult to characterize the Tea Party movement. It has been a nebulous cloud of anger and resentment bent more on opposing progress than actually proposing working solutions.

Now, just as what happened the last time a Democrat was elected, the right-wing extremists have released a Contract [from] America, giving a bit more form to their shifty nature. In this version from the Tea Partiers ... they focus on a few actual issues, among them: the Constitution, cap and trade, a balanced budget, tax reform, fiscal responsibility, government spending, repeal health care reform, energy policy, and an end to earmarks.

Below find the expanded version of this new contract, as well as the response from this particular progressive.

1. Protect the Constitution. Require each bill to identify the specific provision of the Constitution that gives Congress the power to do what the bill does.

The federal [courts] and Supreme Court in the United States are here specifically for this purpose, making this a redundant measure. Nonetheless, it is a principle that is admirable, and Congress should never intentionally draft a bill that would violate the Constitution. Unfortunately, many unconstitutional bills have strong support among the ultraconservative Tea Party movement, including the recent bill defunding the community organizing association ACORN [Association of Community Organizations for Reform Now].

The right-wing extremists have released a Contract [from] America, giving a bit more form to their shifty nature.

Further, the federal courts have been stocked with conservative activist judges since [former president Ronald] Reagan, and the Supreme Court is the most extreme right wing in the history of the nation. This has allowed an unprecedented violation of the Constitution in favor of multinational corporations (including foreign ones) who are now not only granted the rights of an actual person, but can spend unlimited fortunes on political campaigns thanks to a recent decision. I challenge any conservative to show me the passage in the Constitution that allows this.

2. Reject Cap & Trade. Stop costly new regulations that would increase unemployment, raise consumer prices, and weaken the nation's global competitiveness with virtually no impact on global temperatures.

Cap and trade is far too weak to actually force polluters to clean up after themselves. What we need is a system of hard caps, where any industry is forced to reduce their emission levels to what they were at in 2005 within a year's time. Then, mandate cuts in those emission levels by 20% per year.

The science behind anthropogenic global warming is solid. Millions of scientists in over 140 countries with decades of measurements and research prove this. Anyone that denies that our species is directly responsible for some severely negative impacts on our environment is simply rejecting science, and we cannot allow narrow-minded regressives like this to stop us from taking the necessary action to protect our one and only planet. The Tea Party claim that regulations will have no impact in curbing pollution is ludicrous and only demonstrates why such a tiny fraction of scientists are conservative.

3. Demand a Balanced Budget. Begin the constitutional amendment process to require a balanced budget with a two-thirds majority needed for any tax hike.

Everyone wants a balanced budget. The reality to the current situation is this, though: We are in the worst economic downturn since the 1930s, and to stop the Great Recession from turning into another Great Depression, we simply need to run temporary deficits to jump-start the economy. Mandating a two-thirds majority for the simplest of new taxes is not only unconstitutional, it will hamstring Congress from adapting to pressing situations like the one our nation currently faces. Further, it has been tried in California and has had disastrous results, forcing severe cuts in education among other things.

Back to a balanced budget. Where were all the howling voices of condemnation when [former president George W.] Bush doubled the national debt after being handed a surplus from [former president] Bill Clinton? Where were the boisterous complaints when tax cuts for the rich rammed down the throat of America during wartime done by a Republican-controlled Congress caused deficits to balloon? This perhaps demonstrates more than anything how partisan the Tea Partiers are in reality, because if they truly believed in sound fiscal policy instead of borrow and spend fiscal conservativism, they would have had massive demonstrations starting in 2003. Sort of funny how all of sudden these protests cropped up 2 months after a Democrat became president, isn't it? Also, why do so many people at the Tea Parties idolize Ronald Reagan as a great American prophet when he tripled the national debt?

4. Enact Fundamental Tax Reform. Adopt a simple and fair single-rate tax system by scrapping the internal revenue code and replacing it with one that is no longer than 4,543 words— the length of the original Constitution.

Nobody enjoys filling out their tax forms, but it is complicated for a reason: to provide balance to who is allowed deductions. Tax reform is often nothing more than a code phrase for scrapping the progressive income tax in favor of something that will lead to even more devastating wealth consolidation than what has been allowed to take place since Reagan. Class warfare has been waged on the poor for decades, but only when the results of a conservative tax policy that has the top rate at historical lows have come to light recently has the middle class realized that when the rich don't pay their fair share, everyone suffers.

5. Restore Fiscal Responsibility & Constitutionally Limited Government in Washington. Create a blue ribbon task force that engages in a complete audit of federal agencies and programs, assessing their constitutionality and identifying duplication, waste, ineffectiveness, and agencies and programs better left for the states or local authorities, or ripe for wholesale reform or elimination due to our efforts to restore limited government consistent with the US Constitution's meaning.

Looking for increased efficiency and fiscal responsibility is something we can all stand behind, but somehow I doubt Tea Party conservatives would get behind what really needs to be done. See response to #6.

Is the Tea Party Movement Compatible with the Republican Party?

6. End Runaway Government Spending. Impose a statutory cap limiting the annual growth in total federal spending to the sum of the inflation rate plus the percentage of population growth.

The largest piece of discretionary spending in the budget is the military. Including the interest on the national debt incurred by previous borrowing to fund military projects, as well as things hidden in the budget like Iraq War supplements, corporate welfare for research and development, no-bid civilian contractors, and social protections, military-related expenditures are between 40–50% of the annual budget. Nobody will ever be taken seriously when they talk about government spending unless they support massive cuts to the military, and no offense Tea Baggers, but this ain't you.

Further, the most popular cuts in a recent *Economist* poll were foreign aid, agriculture, the environment, and housing, things that only account for a tiny portion of the overall annual budget. It's easy to say you are for cuts, but without specifics, it is just talk.

7. Defund, Repeal, & Replace Government-Run Health Care. Defund, repeal and replace the recently passed government-run health care with a system that actually makes health care and insurance more affordable by enabling a competitive, open, and transparent free market health care and health insurance system that isn't restricted by state boundaries.

The Tea Party "solution" to the health care crisis would do nothing to help the 50 million Americans without health insurance, a rate that is rising rapidly in every state. It would not stop 50,000 people from dying every year due to complications stemming from lack of insurance. It would not stop diabolical corporate practices like denying coverage for such preexisting conditions as domestic violence, being a cop, or taking anti-HIV medications after being raped. It would do nothing to stop the devastating bills that come with a catastrophic illness, the single largest factor in personal bankruptcies and home foreclosures.

As for opening up the insurance system beyond state lines, we all know how well that worked for the credit card companies, who flocked the states with the least amount of consumer protection, and began raking in record profits at everyone's expense. This handicaps individual states from passing laws that are in the interest of their constituents. So much for the illusion of conservatives favoring states' rights.

Everyone knows Tea Party conservatives don't like health care reform, but this is the first time I have seen a declaration to end Medicare and Medicaid too. This is a position even too extreme for the Republicans, who have become increasingly extreme the way it is over the years. At least now everyone now understands the official Tea Party stance on this. Perhaps they would like to abolish Social Security as well.

8. Pass on "All-of-the-Above" Energy Policy. Authorize the exploration of proven energy reserves to reduce our dependence on foreign energy sources from unstable countries and reduce regulatory barriers to all other forms of energy creation, lowering prices and creating competition and jobs.

In order to wean our country off of its addiction to foreign oil, we need to develop energy sources at home that are both renewable and have the least environmental impact. To make this happen, we need to invest enormous sums to develop wind, solar, tidal, and geothermal energy, along with upgrading our transmission network. As the government has given a vast fortune in incentives for big oil to develop infrastructure, and to this day continues to invest 2.5 times the amount in expendable energy sources, the best thing for our nation's future is to develop renewable energy.

Also, since Obama just opened up vast tracts of coastline to offshore drilling, I assume everyone at the Tea Parties strongly and vocally will support that decision, right?

9. Stop the Pork. Place a moratorium on all earmarks until the budget is balanced, and then require a two-thirds majority to pass any earmark.

Earmarks have declined 15.5% this year. Still, rather than speak out in general against earmarks, let the Tea Partiers in the districts who are to receive them be the first to speak out just to prove they are not hypocritical.

10. Stop the Tax Hikes. Permanently repeal all tax hikes, including those to the income, capital gains and death taxes, currently scheduled to begin in 2011.

Although 88% of the people that attend Tea Parties according to a recent poll don't know this, income taxes have declined for 95% of working Americans. Most of that was $300 billion set aside in the American Recovery and Reinvestment Act (stimulus bill), although other tax deductions have come into play as well. In the end, there will be a very modest tax increase on the very rich, and only for income in excess of $500,000. Hardly the doom and gloom message the propagandists on Fox "News" say.

Tea Party Libertarians Are Fundamentally at Odds with Republicans

Glenn Greenwald

Glenn Greenwald is a US lawyer, columnist, blogger, and author.

There's a major political fraud under way: The GOP [the Republican Party] is once again donning [its] libertarian, limited-government masks in order to reinvent itself and, more important, to co-opt the energy and passion of the [libertarian congressman] Ron Paul faction that spawned and sustains the "Tea Party" movement. The party that spat contempt at Paul during the [former president George W.] Bush years and was diametrically opposed to most of his platform now pretends to share his views. Standard-issue Republicans and Ron Paul libertarians are as incompatible as two factions can be—recall that the most celebrated right-wing moment of the 2008 presidential campaign was when Rudy Giuliani all but accused Paul of being an America-hating terrorist-lover for daring to suggest that America's conduct might contribute to Islamic radicalism—yet the Republicans, aided by the media, are pretending that this is one unified, harmonious, "small government" political movement.

The Myth of Republican Belief in Small Government

The Right is petrified that this fraud will be exposed and is thus bending over backwards to sustain the myth. Paul was not only invited to be a featured speaker at the Conservative Political Action Conference [CPAC] but also won its presiden-

Glenn Greenwald, "The GOP's 'Small Government' Tea Party Fraud," *Salon*, February 21, 2010. www.salon.com. Copyright © 2010 by Glenn Greenwald. All rights reserved. Reproduced by permission of Salon Media Group, Inc.

tial straw poll. [Former Alaska governor and 2008 vice presidential candidate] Sarah Palin endorsed Ron Paul's son in the Kentucky Senate race. *National Review* is lavishly praising Paul, while [conservative commentator] Ann Coulter "felt compelled [in her CPAC speech] to give a shout out to Paul mania, saying she agreed with everything he stands for outside of foreign policy—a statement met with cheers." [Conservative radio and television host] Glenn Beck—who literally cheered for the Wall Street bailout and Bush's endlessly expanding surveillance state—now parades around as though he shares the libertarians' contempt for them. *RedState*'s Erick Erickson, defending the new so-called conservative "manifesto," touts the need for Congress to be confined to the express powers of Article I, Section 8, all while lauding a GOP Congress that supported countless intrusive laws—from federalized restrictions on assisted suicide, marriage, gambling, abortion and drugs to intervention in Terri Schiavo's end-of-life state court proceeding—nowhere to be found in that constitutional clause. With the GOP out of power, Fox News suddenly started featuring antigovernment libertarians such as John Stossel and *Reason* magazine commentators, whereas, when Bush was in power, there was no government power too expanded or limitless for Fox propagandists to praise.

This is what Republicans always do. When in power, they massively expand the power of the state in every realm. Deficit spending and the national debt skyrocket. The National Security State is bloated beyond description through wars and occupations, while no limits are tolerated on the Surveillance State. Then, when out of power, they suddenly pretend to rediscover their "small government principles." The very same Republicans who spent the 1990s vehemently opposing Bill Clinton's terrorism-justified attempts to expand government surveillance and executive authority then, once in power, presided over the largest expansion in history of those very same powers. The last eight years of Republican rule was characterized by nothing other than endlessly expanded government power, even as they insisted—both before they were empowered and again now—that they are the standard bearers of government restraint.

> *When in power, [Republicans] . . . massively expand the power of the state in every realm. . . . [W]hen out of power, they suddenly pretend to rediscover their "small government principles."*

Incompatibility with the Tea Party

What makes this deceit particularly urgent for them now is that their only hope for re-branding and re-empowerment lies in a movement—the Tea Partiers—that has been (largely though not exclusively) dominated by libertarians, Paul followers, and other assorted idiosyncratic factions who are hostile to the GOP's actual approach to governing. This is a huge wedge waiting to be exposed—to explode—as the modern GOP establishment and the actual "small-government" libertarians that fuel the Tea Party are fundamentally incompatible. Right-wing mavens like Ann Coulter, Sarah Palin and *National Review* are suddenly feigning great respect for Ron Paul and like-minded activists because they're eager that the sham will be maintained: the blatant sham that the modern GOP and its movement conservatives are a coherent vehicle for those who believe in small government principles. The only evidence of a passionate movement urging GOP resurgence is from people whose views are antithetical to that party. That's the dirty secret which right-wing polemicists are desperately trying to keep suppressed. Credit to Mike Huckabee for acknowledging this core incompatibility by saying he would not attend CPAC because of its "increasing libertarianism."

These fault lines began to emerge when Sarah Palin earlier this month [February 2010] delivered the keynote speech to the national Tea Party conference in Nashville, and stood there spitting out one platitude after the next which Paul-led libertarians despise: from neoconservative war-loving dogma and veneration of Israel to glorification of "War on Terror" domestic powers and the need of the state to enforce Palin's own religious and cultural values. Neocons (who still overwhelmingly dominate the GOP) and Paul-led libertarians are arch enemies, and the social conservatives on whom the GOP depends are barely viewed with greater affection. Sarah Palin and Ron Paul are about as far apart on most issues as one can get; the "Tea Party movement" can't possibly be about supporting each of their worldviews. Moreover, the GOP leadership is currently promising Wall Street even more loyal subservience than Democrats have given in exchange for support, thus bolstering the government/corporate axis which libertarians find so repugnant. And Coulter's manipulative claim that she "agrees with everything [Paul] stands for outside of foreign policy" is laughable; aside from the fact that "foreign policy" is a rather large issue in our political debates (Iraq, Israel, Afghanistan, Iran, Russia), they were on exactly the opposite sides of the most intense domestic controversies of the Bush era: torture, military commissions, habeas corpus, Guantánamo [Bay detention camp], CIA secrecy, telecom immunity, and warrantless eavesdropping.

The very idea that a political party dominated by neocons, warmongers, surveillance fetishists, and privacy-hating social conservatives will be a party of "limited government" is absurd.

Libertarians Seeking Acceptance

Part of why this fraud has been sustainable thus far is that libertarians—like everyone who doesn't view all politics through the mandated, distorting, suffocating Democrat v. GOP prism—are typically dismissed as loons and nuts, and are thus eager for any means of achieving mainstream acceptance. Having the GOP embrace them is one way to achieve that.... Additionally, just as the Paul faction of libertarians is in basic harmony with many progressives on issues of foreign policy and civil liberties, they do subscribe to the standard GOP rhetoric on domestic spending, social programs and the like.

But that GOP limited government rhetoric is simply never matched by that party's conduct, especially when they wield power. The very idea that a political party dominated by neocons, warmongers, surveillance fetishists, and privacy-hating social conservatives will be a party of "limited government" is absurd on its face. There literally is no myth more transparent than the Republican Party's claim to believe in restrained government power. For that reason, it's only a matter of time before the fundamental incompatibility of the "Tea Party movement" and the political party cynically exploiting it is exposed.

The Tea Party Disagrees with Republican Positions on Foreign Policy

Barry Gewen

Barry Gewen has been an editor at the New York Times Book Review *for more than twenty years. He also has written frequently for many other publications.*

Now that the [2010] midterm elections are over and voices of the Tea Party will soon be established in Congress, the movement's views on foreign policy will come under closer scrutiny, and the results may prove surprising, not least to the Tea Partiers themselves. Those views are far from Republican orthodoxy. On some issues, the Tea Partiers will predictably line up with the Republican leadership, but on others they may find they have more in common with Democrats. They may even provide Barack Obama with unexpected support. Those who think Sarah Palin [former governor of Alaska and vice presidential candidate in 2008] speaks for the Tea Party on foreign policy haven't been paying attention.

No Tea Party Foreign Policy

It's hard enough to define Tea Party policies on domestic issues. As Kate Zernike writes in *Boiling Mad: Inside Tea Party America*, the movement "meant different things to different people—even those within the movement could not always agree on what they wanted." But the Tea Party is the soul of rationality and consistency on domestic issues compared to its stand on foreign policy questions. There is simply no there there.

Barry Gewen, "How the Tea Party Is Wrecking Republican Foreign Policy," *New Republic*, December 4, 2010. Copyright © 2010 by Barry Gewen. All rights reserved. Reproduced by permission of The New Republic.

Books on the Tea Partiers, like Zernike's, barely mention foreign policy, and most of the media are no better in their coverage. A search of the Web turns up little more, an occasional blog post or cursory comment, but nothing of any real substance. Probably the most extensive discussion of the subject was written by P.J. O'Rourke, a humorist. Asked if the Tea Party had a foreign policy, Dick Armey, who has made himself one of the movement's stalwarts, responded, "I don't think so." Analysts of the Tea Party's foreign policy are therefore working largely in the dark. Still, one can glimpse occasional flickers of light that permit some extrapolations and tentative conclusions.

Tea Partiers are suspicious of free trade and globalization in general, because they fear a loss of American jobs. Yet the Republican Party has traditionally been the party of free trade.

Immigration and Trade Differences

Take two issues where domestic and foreign policy overlap: immigration and trade. On neither of these questions is the movement in step with Republican Party orthodoxy. With regard to immigration, Tea Partiers often exhibit a hostility that shades into nativism. Remember Sharron Angle's endorsement of Phoenix's hard-line sheriff, Joe Arpaio: every state, she said, should have a sheriff like Joe Arpaio. Citing a *New York Times* poll, Zernike notes that 82 percent of Tea Partiers think illegal immigration is a "very serious" problem, compared to 60 percent of the general public. Yet the corporate sector of the Republican Party has always shown sympathy for increased immigration, and often seems willing to look the other way over illegal immigration. The more immigrants, the greater the competition for jobs, the lower the wage costs for business. Besides, someone has to mow the lawn and look after the kids.

Similar forces are at play in the case of trade. Tea Partiers are suspicious of free trade and globalization in general, because they fear a loss of American jobs. Yet the Republican Party has traditionally been the party of free trade. The Tea Partiers will find their closest allies on this issue among Democrats, especially trade unionists. We just saw what the future politics of trade will look like when President Obama had trouble concluding a free trade pact with South Korea, originally approved by George W. Bush in 2007. A coalition of Democrats and Tea Partiers inside and outside of Congress opposed it, despite its potential to boost our economy and strengthen crucial alliances in Asia.

In truth, on both immigration and trade, the Tea Partiers are in favor of more government, not less, putting them at odds with Republican Party laissez-faire instincts. However they may feel about the evil of deficits, Tea Partiers are not libertarians. By majorities of almost two-to-one, they support Social Security and Medicare. As Scott Rasmussen and Douglas Schoen write in their book *Mad as Hell: [How the Tea Party Movement Is Fundamentally Remaking Our Two-Party System]*, "it would be a profound mistake to say that they are an adjunct of the GOP."

Larger Differences on Other Foreign Policy Issues

But it's on questions of America's role in the world that the divisions between Tea Partiers and standard-issue Republicans begin to look like chasms. The key figures here are the Pauls, Ron and Rand, longtime congressman and recently elected senator, father and son. Ron Paul has been called "the Tea Party's brain," its "intellectual godfather"; Rand Paul, by virtue of his election victory, has made himself a powerful, perhaps the most powerful, Tea Party spokesman on the hill.

The Pauls' positions on foreign policy are not identical, but the links between them are more than genetic. In a recent statement for *Foreign Policy* magazine, Ron Paul called for an end to "the disastrous wars in Iraq and Afghanistan." He went on: "We cannot talk about the budget deficit and spiraling domestic spending without looking at the costs of maintaining an American empire of more than 700 military bases in more than 120 foreign countries." And like father, like son. Rand Paul has said that "part of the reason we are bankrupt as a country is that we are fighting so many foreign wars and have so many military bases around the world." He opposes what he calls "a blank check for the military."

It's on questions of America's role in the world that the divisions between Tea Partiers and standard-issue Republicans begin to look like chasms.

Tea Party Commonalities with Democrats

These freshly invigorated voices within the Republican Party are already finding common cause with doves inside the Democratic Party. Ron Paul has joined with Barney Frank in calling for the withdrawal of troops from Afghanistan and Iraq, as well as from Germany, Japan, and South Korea. "We don't need to be the world's policeman," Paul said, echoing the Vietnam war protesters of an earlier era.

Hawkish Republicans have taken note. Casting a suspicious eye at the Tea Partiers, John McCain has said, "I worry a lot about the rise of protectionism and isolationism in the Republican Party." There was a truce within the party until the elections, but now, as Richard Viguerie warned, "a massive, almost historic battle for the heart and soul of the Republican Party begins." Onlookers can expect to hear a great deal of name-calling in coming months as charges of "isolationist" and "imperialist" fly back and forth.

Sarah Palin vs. Ron Paul

At the center of this battle, of course, is Sarah Palin. She has allied herself firmly with the Republican hawks, opposing any cuts in defense spending and generally calling for a more activist and interventionist America throughout the world. She is on record in support of an attack on Iran. To much of the press and the punditocracy, she is the darling of the Tea Partiers, but that's not how it looks to many inside the movement, and if you want to hear the worst of the vituperation aimed her way, you should look not in the direction of liberals and Democrats, but at the Ron Paul wing of the Tea Party movement. Accused of hijacking the movement for the neoconservatives, she is called "a wolf in sheep's clothing," "simplistic," "senseless and deranged," "close-minded," "arrogant," "a neocon Stepford wife."

She and [conservative commentator] Glenn Beck, another hijacker, are "duplicitous and deceiving whores of the global establishment, practiced at fooling well-meaning followers into betraying their own interests." And maybe worst of all, "just like Obama and the Democrat version of Bush neocons."

. . .

Unsurprisingly, a considerable amount of the name-calling comes down to Israel. It can't be said that Palin has taken a strong stand on Israel—a more appropriate characterization would be that she out-Netanyahus [Israeli Prime Minister] Benjamin Netanyahu: "I believe that the Jewish settlements should be allowed to be expanded upon, because that population of Israel is going to grow. More and more Jewish people will be flocking to Israel in the days and weeks and months ahead. And I don't think that the Obama administration has any right to tell Israel that the Jewish settlements cannot expand."

Such sentiments win no applause from the Tea Partiers aligned with Ron Paul. He has repeatedly condemned Israeli policies, often in the harshest terms. One of his staffers declared that, "By far the most powerful lobby in Washington of the bad sort is the Israeli government." Paul's opponents inside and outside the Tea Party see undertones of anti-Semitism in his positions, or worse, though John Podhoretz, the editor of *Commentary*, gives him something of a pass: "I'm inclined to think that Paul, who is not the most careful and prudent of speakers, is not an anti-Semite." But he adds that Paul does follow in a tradition of American isolationism that, in its history, has been "a hotbed of classic and unambiguous anti-Semitism throughout the 20th century."

One of the odder twists in this intramural debate—and possibly a sign of things to come—was an idea recently floated by Congressman Eric Cantor to remove aid to Israel from the foreign operations budget. It could be seen as a preemptive step to preserve aid to Israel at a time when his party, under the increasing influence of the Tea Party movement, is less sympathetic to foreign aid and defense spending, and less automatically supportive of Israel. The plan went nowhere as influential groups like AIPAC [American Israel Political Affairs Committee, a pro-Israel lobby group] roundly opposed it, and Cantor quickly backtracked. But as the only Jewish Republican congressman, he may have been more sensitive to the drift of the Republican Party than other Jewish leaders.

By the same token, if the president proposes cuts in military spending, there will probably be Tea Partiers ready to support him. If Obama decides to speed up withdrawals from Iraq and Afghanistan, he could find Republican backers for that, too. And most controversial of all, if he attempts to put some distance between the United States and Benjamin Netanyahu's government, he may discover that as the Tea Party movement extends its sway, his political bedfellows have become stranger and stranger.

The Tea Party Will Cause Republicans to Lose the 2012 Presidential Election

Mark Shields

Mark Shields is a writer and political commentator who has appeared on various television news shows, including CNN's Capital Gang *and public television's* NewsHour with Jim Lehrer.

For the first and only time in a remarkable political career—which began in 1966 when he captured a "safe" Democratic state legislative seat and included winning campaigns for the state Senate, for lieutenant governor, for two terms as governor and then nine terms to the U.S. House—Mike Castle, on a Tuesday night in September 2010, lost an election.

In the crowd of admirers who heard him concede, there were more than a few tears, some disbelief and a ton of anger.

Joe Meloy, 76, a veteran Republican activist in Delaware, was solemn: "Mike Castle is totally principled, the finest gentleman in the world." And the Tea Party–Rush Limbaugh–Sarah Palin–backed opponent who defeated him, Christine O'Donnell? "She's a flake—a complete whack job."

There was understandable fury at [conservative radio personality Rush] Limbaugh's ugly smear on his Election Day radio show that Castle in 2008 had nefariously supported sending a resolution calling for the impeachment of President George W. Bush to the Democratically controlled House Judiciary Committee. Limbaugh deliberately chose to ignore the fact that two of Bush's strongest fellow Texas conservatives, Reps. Kevin Brady and Sam Johnson, along with the senior

Mark Shields, "How the Tea Party Will Change the GOP," Creators.com, September 18, 2010. www.creators.com. Copyright © 2010 by Mark Shields. All rights reserved. Reproduced by permission of Creators Syndicate.

Republican on the House Rules Committee, California Rep. David Dreier, voted with Castle to send the impeachment resolution to legislative oblivion, where as they intended, it died a silent death.

Embracing Extremist Agendas

It must first be acknowledged that the Tea Party has brought both dramatically increased numbers and enormous energy to the 2010 Republican primaries. True, with Castle's defeat, Democrat Chris Coons is now heavily favored to win the Delaware U.S. Senate seat Democrats had privately conceded to Castle before O'Donnell pulled her upset. But as Democrats learned in the 1970s, the newcomers' energy and enthusiasm comes with a stiff price for the party.

Forty years ago, the issues and the causes and the constituencies were different: fierce, largely youthful, opposition to the Vietnam War, uncompromising supporters of abortion rights and gay rights, and environmental activists.

But the same fever of abolitionist morality—seen in the current Tea Party—characterized the "New People" to politics who then, as now, were free of self-doubt and brimming with passion and a sense of their own rectitude.

Ronald Reagan's "80 percent rule"—that someone who votes with you 80 percent of the time is an ally and a friend and NOT a 20 percent traitor—is heresy to all Tea Party types. In their unreflective conviction, cooperation on any issue with those on the other side is disloyal and compromise of any kind is treasonous.

After the "New People"—the insurgents, whether on the Democratic left or the Republican right—prove by their energy and numbers they can defeat a targeted incumbent in a primary, other elected politicians and party leaders are terrified. They quickly sue for peace with the activists, embracing their agendas and being overly careful never to make them angry or even unhappy.

This was the case from 1972 forward in the Democratic Party presidential nominating contests. Candidates relentlessly, even shamelessly, solicited the blessings, if not the endorsements, of the antiwar, pro-choice, gay rights and environmentalist lobbies. A veto from one of them could cripple a Democrat's White House prospects.

Watching the 2012 GOP [Republican Party] pander to the Tea Party will be dispiriting and politically damaging—and could well be the key to . . . President Barack Obama winning a second White House term.

Reelecting President Obama

Look for the 2012 Republican presidential field to totally embrace the Tea Party program. The only place you will find the word bipartisan will be in the dictionary. Candidates, ignoring the contradictions in their positions, will swear allegiance to a balanced federal budget while simultaneously, and hypocritically, championing trillions more in tax cuts for the most affluent.

Watching the 2012 GOP [Republican Party] pander to the Tea Party will be dispiriting and politically damaging—and could well be the key to the beleaguered incumbent, President Barack Obama, winning a second White House term. Remember: If that happens, you heard it here first.

CHAPTER 4

What Is the Future of the Tea Party Movement?

Chapter Preface

Sarah Palin, the charismatic former governor of Alaska and Republican vice presidential candidate in the 2008 presidential race, has become the public face of the Tea Party, according to many media sources. Although she currently holds no public office, Palin has positioned herself through speeches, tweets, and other public statements as a highly visible commentator on national politics—a commentator who has lent support for Tea Party causes while at the same time seeking to put her stamp on Tea Party goals. For better or for worse, Palin appears to have linked herself with the Tea Party, perhaps even considering becoming a Tea Party candidate in the 2012 presidential election.

Throughout 2010, Sarah Palin appeared and spoke at numerous Tea Party rallies. Palin first aligned herself with the Tea Party in February 2010, when she was the keynote speaker at a national Tea Party convention in Nashville, Tennessee, that was organized by one of the major Tea Party groups, the Tea Party Nation. Although Palin's presence at the convention was controversial, both because she was paid a relatively high fee of $100,000 for her speech and because many grassroots Tea Party supporters didn't like the idea of anointing a national leader, her speech attracted widespread media attention and helped to showcase Palin and the Tea Party as formidable voices in national political circles.

In her February speech, Palin promoted the Tea Party's broad principles such as lower taxes, limited government, and strict adherence to the Constitution, and she assailed President Barack Obama and Democrats in Congress. However, she also introduced other ideas that so far had not been part of the Tea Party agenda and that are more closely associated with establishment Republicans. These included arguments for a strong military defense and aggressive antiterrorism efforts—

causes that many Republicans hope to protect from the Tea Party's demands to cut federal spending.

Sarah Palin continued to keep a high profile as a Tea Party celebrity later in 2010, and she endorsed dozens of Tea Party candidates in the fall 2010 midterm elections. Although a couple of her endorsed candidates lost, Palin's support appeared to help many Tea Party politicians win elected office. Six of her selected Senate candidates won in the November elections, including Tea Party notables Rand Paul from Kentucky and Marco Rubio from Florida, and at least twenty-two of her candidates for the House of Representatives were elected. In two important Senate races, however, in Nevada and Delaware respectively, Palin-supported candidates Sharron Angle and Christine O'Donnell lost. Shortly after the November elections, Palin urged Republicans to come together with the Tea Party to create a smaller federal government and support the private sector.

The main debate surrounding Sarah Palin in early 2011 was whether she will run as a candidate for either the Republican or a possible third-party nomination in the upcoming 2012 presidential election. Many commentators saw Palin's February 2010 Tea Party speech as a clear effort to co-opt the Tea Party and a first step toward positioning herself for 2012. Later, in speeches and web videos, Palin hinted about a possible presidential bid as a third-party, Tea Party candidate. In numerous appearances, for example, Palin praised the Tea Party as a legitimate grassroots political movement and joked about her presidential ambitions. Many establishment Republicans, however, fear her entrance into presidential politics because they fear she would be too polarizing to be a viable Republican candidate against President Barack Obama. Many political experts have suggested, too, that she could divide the Republican vote as a third-party candidate, giving the Democrats a better chance to win another presidential term in 2012. However, some commentators have suggested that it might be possible for the Tea Party to push a presidential candidate like Sarah Palin in the early Iowa, New Hampshire, and South Carolina primaries, and in that way create an unstoppable momentum that could lead to a presidential nomination.

The idea of Sarah Palin as a Tea Party presidential candidate is only one of the possible directions the Tea Party might take in coming months and years. Other ideas about the future of the Tea Party and its effect on national politics are the subject of the viewpoints in this chapter.

The 2010 Midterm Elections Begin a Period of Increased Tea Party Activism

Jennifer Levitz, Cameron McWhirter, and Douglas A. Blackmon

Jennifer Levitz, Cameron McWhirter, and Douglas A. Blackmon are writers for the Wall Street Journal, *a prominent US business and financial newspaper.*

Tea-party leaders, cheering as some of their movement's most prominent figures won U.S. Senate seats in Kentucky and Florida, said Tuesday's [November 2, 2010] elections were only the beginning of their quest to transform government.

"Things look good for tonight," said Jenny Beth Martin, national coordinator of the Tea Party Patriots, an umbrella group that says it has 2,800 local affiliates around the country. "No one in this movement is stopping today. This is not an endgame. This is just a beginning."

A Major Force in Congress

Tea-party victors included Republican Rand Paul, who claimed the Senate seat in Kentucky, and the GOP's [Republican Party's] Marco Rubio, who defeated former Gov. Charlie Crist and Rep. Kendrick Meek in Florida's three-way race for Senate.

Movement losers included Christine O'Donnell, the Republican Senate candidate in Delaware, whose comments about witchcraft embarrassed some in the movement, and Republican Carl Paladino, who lost his bid for governor of New York.

Jennifer Levitz, Cameron McWhirter, and Douglas A. Blackmon, "As Races End, Tea Party Plans for Next Phase," *Wall Street Journal*, November 4, 2010. Reprinted by permission of Wall Street Journal, Copyright © 2010 Dow Jones & Company, Inc. All Rights Reserved Worldwide. License number 2670910729158.

What Is the Future of the Tea Party Movement?

Early results signaled that despite some losses, the movement was on its way to becoming a major force in Washington and on the national political landscape. Ahead is a chaotic period as the movement's factions compete to set the agenda and influence the ranks of new members of Congress.

Despite some losses [in the 2010 midterm elections], the [tea-party] movement [is] . . . on its way to becoming a major force in Washington and on the national political landscape.

One of the most prominent national tea-party groups, Tea Party Patriots, announced plans for a summit of newly minted officials in two weeks while Mr. Paul said he would convene his own similar gathering as soon as possible.

In an op-ed article in Wednesday's editions of the *Wall Street Journal*, major tea-party figure Sen. Jim DeMint (R., S.C.) called on newly elected officials to hew to the movement's priorities as they decamp to Washington. "When you are in Washington, remember what the voters back home want—less government and more freedom," wrote Mr. DeMint. "Put on your boxing gloves. The fight begins today."

Ms. Martin said Tea Party Patriots is finalizing plans for a summit and "orientation" Nov. 14 in Washington for all freshman members of Congress. Newly elected officials will meet "face to face" with 200 or more local tea-party coordinators from around the country, she said. Her group is working on a legislative agenda to present then. The focus: Balance the federal budget; and repeal "100 percent repeal" of the health-care overhaul.

"We're going to talk to them about what we expect from them," she said, "and what they can expect from us if they don't uphold our core values."

Across the country, tea-party activists gathered in churches, living rooms, fraternal lodges and bars awaiting the results of more than a year of grassroots organizing. Almost uniformly they said they remained wary of everyone in Washington—including their own candidates.

In LaGrange, Ga., 65 miles south of Atlanta, the local tea-party group already was organizing a postelection letter campaign to remind new officials to not cozy up to the Republican establishment.

The focus [of the Tea Party Patriots, one of the most prominent tea-party groups]: Balance the federal budget; and repeal "100 percent repeal" of the health-care overhaul.

"Come January," said Ellen Gilmore, a 69-year-old retired dental hygienist, "We'll be all over them like dew in the cotton fields."

In Kentucky, Mr. Paul, the son of libertarian icon Rep. Ron Paul (R., Texas) led his Democratic opponent, Jack Conway, 56% to 44% with 97% of Kentucky precincts reporting, according to data provided by the Associated Press.

"There is a tea-party tidal wave coming to Washington," said Mr. Paul, a 47-year-old eye surgeon, after voting Tuesday morning at an elementary school.

"Both parties let us down," he said. He added that, if elected, his first objective would be to secure a constitutional amendment requiring a balanced federal budget.

Mr. Paul said Tuesday that he won't compromise his positions regarding the deficit once in Washington and plans to organize his own meeting of victorious tea-party candidates to plan the best way to achieve the movement's agenda.

Three Symbolic Races

In Nevada, leaders of the Tea Party Express, which poured more than $1 million into Republican Sharron Angle's bid to unseat Democratic Senate Majority Leader Harry Reid, holed up in a "war room" in a suite at the Aria casino and hotel on the Las Vegas strip.

The group endorsed Ms. Angle in April when she was polling at 5% in the Republican primary and appeared to have no shot at her party's nomination. Tea Party Express, another prominent national tea-party group, spent heavily on advertising and assigned operatives to operate a separate campaign on Ms. Angle's behalf during the primary.

The race now is the marquee battle for the organization, which also heavily backed Republican Senate candidate Joe Miller in Alaska and Ms. O'Donnell in Delaware.

In late polls during the campaign, Ms. Angle had inched ahead. But in the final days, Mr. Reid was getting aid from Democrats across the country for a huge get-out-the-vote effort to mobilize loyal supporters. "There's no question this race is iconic and symbolic of the tea party movement versus the establishment," said Tea Party Express spokesman Levi Russell. "There will be many victories tonight. We just hope this will be one of those victories. The next election cycle starts tomorrow and we'll move over to that."

Editor's note: All three Tea Party candidates—Sharron Angle, Joe Miller, and Christine O'Donnell—ultimately lost their Senate races.

The Tea Party Will Be Betrayed by Corporate-Funded Politicians

Dave Johnson

Dave Johnson is a fellow at Campaign for America's Future—a progressive think tank—and a senior fellow at another progressive group, Renew California.

Tea Party members hate Wall Street bailouts, trade deals like NAFTA [North American Free Trade Agreement], job outsourcing, giant corporations buying laws, government spending, and elites telling the rest of us what to do. But there is no question that their candidates—many of them wealthy corporatists themselves—are funded by big corporations (even foreign oil companies) and Wall Street. So the question is, once in Congress will they vote with their base or their owners? And when they vote with the people who bought them, what will Tea Party members do about it?

Trade, Outsourcing, and Bailouts

Tea Party members want to be able to buy things that are "Made in America" in stores again. I have yet to meet a Tea Party supporter who doesn't absolutely hate NAFTA, WTO [World Trade Organization] and other one-sided "free trade" agreements. They say these treaties "violate our sovereignty." But Tea Party candidates are funded by groups like the Chamber of Commerce and others who are the drivers of these "free trade" policies that close American factories and send jobs out of the country. This does not bode well for these candidates voting the way Tea Party members expect them to if they are elected.

Dave Johnson, "What Will Tea Party Members Do When Their Politicians Betray Them?" OurFuture.org, October 26, 2010. www.ourfuture.org. Copyright © 2010 by Dave Johnson. All rights reserved. Reproduced by permission of Campaign For America's Future.

Tea Party members are [also] astonished when they learn that the government gives companies tax breaks that encourage companies to send jobs away. But just a month ago a bill to do something about this was filibustered in the Senate by a unanimous Republican caucus. One thing about Tea Party candidates—they're also unanimously Republicans. Does anyone other than Tea Party members really think the Tea Party candidates are going to go against the now-unanimous Republican support for these outsourcing incentives if elected? Tea Party candidate Scott Brown didn't after he was elected.

[Finally,] if there is one thing that unites all Tea Party members, it is hatred of the [former president George W.] Bush Bank Bailouts (except they think these passed under Obama). But this is an area where their leaders will almost certainly stand with the banks, because that's where the money is—their campaign money to be precise. The other day I wrote about . . . [how] one Wall Street hedge fund manager is spending up to $1 million (pocket change) on a front group to elect a Tea Party candidate and unseat a congressman who sponsored a couple of Wall Street reform bills.

Government Spending

Will Tea Party politicians vote to balance the budget? *Really?* Their members certainly expect them to. But like so many misinformed Americans, Tea Party members think the government spends most of its money on welfare and foreign aid. This is why Tea Party candidates refuse to specify just *what* spending they will cut to balance the budget.

So when they get into office will they really cut spending—where the spending really *is?* There are plenty of reasons to think they won't. The first and foremost reason is they are funded by people like the Chamber of Commerce who really, really want that spending to keep flowing. This is why Republicans increased government spending and deficits so much the last time they were in charge. In fact, there are reasons to think they'll *increase* spending. For example, they hate health care reform, but if they really vote to repeal it they will *increase* the deficit, because the reform cuts the projected deficits by at least $138 billion.

The members might supply the votes, but the big corporations . . . are the ones supplying the money and organization.

But the bloated, huge, vast, overcoming military budget might be worth a look. We spend more on military than every other country *combined*. (Total military-related spending actually pretty closely matched the deficit this year.) What do you think the odds are that the Tea Party politicians will cut the military budget?

Foreign Oil

Tea Party members understand that our addiction to foreign oil is harmful. We spend more than $300 billion a year on foreign oil—much of it sent to the Middle East (MUSLIMS!)—and need to find alternative sources of energy. But Koch [Industries] is the primary organizer, supporter, funder, and everything of the Tea Party, as well as much of the so-called "conservative movement." But Koch [Industries] is mostly about oil, not representative government. This is why they directly fund or set up front groups to support climate denial or oppose transit projects, alternative energy, even energy conservation. So don't expect Tea Party leaders to do anything—anything—that Koch [Industries] doesn't want them to do.

What Happens When Tea Party Members Are Betrayed?

It's pretty clear that the Tea Party members are being set up for a big disappointment. There is little chance that the politicians they are supporting are going to do what the members think they're going to do once in office. The members might supply the votes, but the big corporations behind so many of the things that the Tea Party members hate are the ones supplying the money and organization. These politicians, once in office, will understand that the big money can go after them just as well as it went for them this time, if they don't do what they're told by their big corporate funders. But on the other hand, there will be lucrative lobbying jobs waiting for them if they play along. They are going to disappoint the Tea Party members, no question. What will Tea Party members do then?

The Tea Party Will Survive Only as a Republican Party Faction

Matt Steinglass

Matt Steinglass (also known as M.S.) is a correspondent for the Economist, *a weekly newsmagazine based in London.*

Tea-party candidates have won 24 out of their 51 serious primary races, by [*Slate* magazine journalist] Dave Weigel's tally, and a fair number of them will surely make it into Congress. Most liberals are excited by the Far-Right candidates' wins, figuring they'll lead to fewer GOP [Republican] takeovers in November [2010]. [*Mother Jones* magazine reporter] Kevin Drum endorses a "heighten the contradictions" strategy: "the GOP is irrevocably committed to the undiluted Fox/Limbaugh/Drudge party line, and there's no going back. They're either going to stand or fall on that. So I say: let 'em do it. No excuses, no scapegoats." [Author] Matthew Yglesias cautions that "ultimately, the two-party system operates near equilibrium, and so the internal state of both parties counts. It's better for progressives and better for the country for Republicans to field strong, reasonable candidates." Meanwhile, centrist conservative Ross Douthat hopes Christine O'Donnell's win in Delaware, which will likely lead to a Democratic win in the Senate race, hastens a Republican return towards the centre: "If O'Donnell's likely general-election fate becomes a cautionary tale about the limits of caring only about ideological purism, then the lessons of Delaware in 2010 might serve the party in good stead come Iowa and New Hampshire in 2012." And pro-Obama post-conservative Andrew Sullivan who's hoped for years that the excesses of

Matt Steinglass, "The Future of the Tea-Party Movement," *Economist*, September 16, 2010. Copyright © 2010 by Matt Steinglass. All rights reserved. Reproduced by permission of The Economist.

[former President George W.] Bush-era neoconservatism would drive the party back towards the centre, only to see it yaw eagerly rightward, is having trouble finding any higher registers on the freak-out scale: "(T)he idea of these people running foreign policy on the basis of religious doctrine, Greater Israel, institutionalized torture and anti-Muslim bigotry, is terrifying."

The tea-party movement has made the smart move of organising as a faction within the Republican Party, evading the eternal doom that [usually] befalls third parties.

A Lasting Impact?

How terrifying is it? One thing I'm constantly struck by with the tea-party movement is its similarity to other upstart right-wing rejectionist political movements around the world that have gained sudden tremendous vote shares, such as Ross Perot's United We Stand America, Pim Fortuyn's List in the Netherlands or Vladimir Zhirinovsky's briefly threatening Liberal-Democratic Party in Russia. One problem such parties tend to have is staffing issues: They can't find enough solid candidates, and tend to wind up nominating a large proportion of flamboyant goofballs who flame out rather quickly. This is likely to be the case with candidates like Ms O'Donnell, Nevada's Sharron Angle, and the new tea-party nominee in New York's race for governor, Carl Paladino.

> "We are mad as hell," Mr. Paladino said in a halting but exuberant victory speech in Buffalo shortly after 11 p.m. "New Yorkers are fed up. Tonight the ruling class knows. They have seen it now. There is a people's revolution. The people have had enough."

Apparently you are allowed to talk about a people's revolution against the ruling class in American politics, so long as you're a real-estate millionaire running as a Republican.

It's possible that the tea-party movement will have a more lasting impact than parties like Mr Perot's, which fizzled by the late 1990s, or Mr Fortuyn's, which flamed out of existence within a year or two of seizing some of the largest vote totals in the country. For one thing, the tea-party movement has made the smart move of organising as a faction within the Republican Party, evading the eternal doom that [usually] befalls third parties in the American system. For another, it is not too closely tied to a single charismatic personality, though a split between Sarah Palin [former governor of Alaska and vice presidential candidate in 2008] and any large segment of the movement might do some damage. And third, it runs no risk of actually wielding power for several years. Pim Fortuyn's List evaporated into incoherence when it made the mistake of joining the ruling coalition, and being forced to craft policies and take positions its followers might dislike. By organising as a faction within the minority party, with a president in office who is guaranteed to excite its followers' rage for at least two more years, the tea-party movement has ensured it can drum up votes for quite some time on the basis of opposition to taxes and proclamations that "the people have had enough."

The Tea Party Will Soon Be Absorbed by the Republican Party

Doyle McManus

Doyle McManus is a Washington columnist for the Los Angeles Times, *reporting on national and international issues from Washington for more than twenty-five years.*

The Tea Party movement is rapidly becoming just another faction of the national Republican Party.

Originally a grassroots expression of anger at both parties, Tea Party groups eyed Democrats and Republicans with suspicion. And the parties were skeptical of the movement, too.

But in recent months, the GOP's [Republican Party's] natural election-year appetite for voters, campaign volunteers and donors has caused the Republicans to take a more welcoming approach, and the Tea Partiers have responded.

Rep. Michele Bachmann, R-Minn., the Sarah Palin [referring to the former governor of Alaska who is a Tea Party supporter] of the House, formed an official Tea Party Caucus on Capitol Hill. Within three days, 42 members of Congress had signed up, all conservative Republicans.

The group won an almost-instant blessing from House Republican leader John A. Boehner, R-Ohio, who described his own experiences at Tea Party rallies with near-religious enthusiasm.

"Last Labor Day weekend, there were 18,000 people about a mile from my home—18,000 people!" Boehner said.

"These folks are the tip of an iceberg," Boehner went on. "We should listen to them, we should work with them and we should walk amongst them."

Doyle McManus, "Will GOP Swallow the Tea Party?" Statesman.com, July 27, 2010. www.statesman.com. Copyright © 2010. All rights reserved. Reproduced by permission of the Los Angeles Times.

The Republican Party Needs the Tea Party

In a midterm election year [2010], when turnout is hard to drum up, it's easy to see why Republicans are eager to harness the zeal. Just 18 months ago, the GOP was flat on its back. In some polls, fewer than 25 percent of voters admitted to being Republicans.

For the GOP, the Tea Party isn't just a potential source of new voters and campaign volunteers; it's a vehicle for rebranding and redemption. Before the Tea Party, the GOP was a tired old organization, financed largely by business lobbyists, that voted repeatedly for deficit spending. Now, to hear Boehner and his lieutenants describe it, the Republican Party is the fully reformed instrument of a virtuous grassroots anti-deficit movement.

That transformation has required something of a Faustian bargain [referring to something done for present gain without regard for the future]. In Nevada and Kentucky, Tea Party activists helped hard-right conservatives in Republican Senate primaries defeat candidates the party's establishment considered more likely to win in November's general election. But that unhappiness is forgotten now, at least officially.

At this point, the Tea Party agenda and the Republican Party agenda have largely merged.

For the GOP, the Tea Party isn't just a potential source of new voters and campaign volunteers; it's a vehicle for rebranding and redemption.

Tea Party activists say they're angry about federal spending, the deficit, the growth of federal government power and President Barack Obama's health care plan. Republican leaders say pretty much the same things.

For Republicans who want to broaden their party's appeal, the good news is that Tea Party activists are concerned mostly about fiscal issues, not the social and religious issues that have driven some independents away from the GOP.

The bad news is that they rank unemployment well below the deficit on their list of concerns—the opposite of most voters.

And, of course, the Tea Party, like any grassroots movement, includes its share of racists, xenophobes and extremists, which is one reason Bachmann's Tea Party Caucus attracted only 40 of the 115 members of the House's existing conservative caucus, the Republican Study Committee.

The Republican leadership, by embracing the Tea Party message, has brought a movement that was once proudly nonpartisan ever deeper inside the conventional-politics tent.

Absorbing the Tea Party into the Republican Party

On the Tea Party side, the movement is still divided among those who want to jump whole hog into Republican politics and those who want to steer clear of traditional party allegiance.

"You need to be part of a party to get candidates elected," said Mark A. Skoda, a Tea Party activist from Memphis, Tenn., who helped found the National Tea Party Federation. "Standing out there with signs doesn't get anything done.

"I know I'll get some hate mail for that," he added. "There are people in the movement who disagree with me. Make sure you say I'm not a spokesman for the Tea Party—because there is no spokesman for the Tea Party."

He praised Bachmann and other GOP leaders for seeking Tea Party support.

"We're not antagonistic toward the Republican Party," he said. "We want to hold the Republican Party accountable. We want to be a change agent for the Republican Party."

That's already happened—in both directions. Both parties, Tea and Republican, have already changed each other.

The Tea Party, by showing up at rallies and polling places, has strengthened those in the GOP who want to energize the conservative base with a campaign that focuses on cutting the deficit and repealing Obama's health care law. The Republican leadership, by embracing the Tea Party message, has brought a movement that was once proudly nonpartisan ever deeper inside the conventional-politics tent.

Which is more likely to absorb the other? That's easy. One isn't an organization; it has two years of experience, no national structure and no real fund-raising operation. The other has operated since 1854, has built a formidable national organization and has survived electoral disaster more than once.

The history of American politics is littered with grassroots movements that challenged existing parties, only to be co-opted and absorbed by them. The only thing new about the Tea Party is that it arose in an age when communications and politics move at lightning speed. Yes, it's streaking across the Republican sky like a comet, but look fast; it may not be there long.

The Tea Party Must Take Over the Republican Party to Succeed

James R. Keena

James R. Keena is a Tea Party activist and speaker; author of the books We've Been Had: How Obama and the Radicals Conned Middle Class America *and* Insurrection Resurrection: A Novel of Political and Religious Satire; *and creator of the website PathlessLand.net.*

Assume, for the purpose of this discussion, that the Tea Party movement continues to significantly influence political outcomes through the 2010 primaries and general elections.

In other words, assume that conservative-leaning candidates win their primaries, that Big Government apologists are defeated in the general election, and that the U.S. House of Representatives is snatched back from the radicals.

What then for the Tea Party movement?

Are the Tea Party tactics of the past 18 months sufficient for continued success in the future? Do we proceed with more rallies of sign-toting and fist-shaking patriots? Do we propagate more speeches and e-mails invoking patriotic icons, anecdotes, and imagery? Do we indulge in more wistful longing for oldies-but-goodies like [former president Ronald] Reagan and a Contract with America? Do we humor more high-profile celebrity, political, and media hangers-on who prove daily that Tea Party success has a thousand vicarious mothers?

None of these tactics are sufficient for future success, even though they contributed to our success in the past. Past is not

James R. Keena, "The Future of the Tea Party Movement," thelandofthefree.net, September 16, 2010. www.thelandofthefree.net. Copyright © 2010 by James R. Keena. All rights reserved. Reproduced by permission of the author.

prologue for the Tea Party movement. Widespread success in November [2010] will cause our political circumstance to be very different. When conservatives retake the U.S. House of Representatives, we will no longer be just a boisterous horde outside the castle; we will be a coterie among the King's court. The stark reality of our accomplishments will necessitate a different strategy for the Tea Party movement. This [viewpoint] proposes such a strategy.

A Conservative Army

First, let's acknowledge that the Tea Party movement has thus far accomplished things that were both extraordinary and necessary. The movement has invigorated a grassroots, boots-on-the-ground army of passionate conservative activists. This is something that the feckless Republican Party, which has been the putative flag-bearer of conservatism, has been utterly incapable of inspiring. The Republican Party, because of its stodgy, wishy-washy, misdirected political inertia, is not yet even fully attuned to the limited-government tsunami that has cascaded out of the Tea Party movement. More will be said about that shortly.

The Tea Party movement has also become the counterpoint to the Left's radical boots-on-the-ground coalition that includes termites like ACORN [Association of Organizers for Reform Now] (or whatever they've disguised themselves as now), Organizing for America, and MoveOn.org [progressive organizations]. Tea Partiers, to their considerable credit, accomplished this without the corrupting billions of rogue [progressive billionaire George] Soros-like backers or the endless manna granted by foundations and government agencies that typically support left-leaning activists. The Tea Party movement is truly a grassroots phenomenon, unlike the ersatz publicly and institutionally funded Astroturf organizations of the Left.

Emotionally, the Tea Party movement has infused conservatives with an energy that seemed unimaginable just 18 months ago. It has reintroduced the concept of limited government into mainstream American political conversation. It has taught politicians of all stripes that "We the People" is no longer a trite patriotic anachronism, but rather the battle cry of a grassroots electoral tiger with razor-sharp fangs.

It is one thing to successfully awaken and energize the conservative tiger.... It is entirely another thing ... to channel that energy into a ... path forward for the country.

Creating a Mandate

However, the success of the Tea Party movement thus far has certain inherent limitations. It is one thing to successfully awaken and energize the conservative tiger, which will certainly be manifested as an electoral blood-letting in November. It is entirely another thing, though, to channel that energy into a defined and executable path forward for the country. The Tea Party momentum from the impending electoral victories in 2010 must be codified into a widely embraceable mandate. It is only through such a mandate that the movement can emerge from the 2012 elections as an executable political revolution.

Said another way, it is one thing to shout "throw the bums out" and to proceed to do just that in the voting booths in November. It is entirely another thing, though, to elect politicians to stand in place of the evicted bums who can lead with courage, audacity, and steadfast commitment to limited government. Such is the kind of leadership that Republicans have not recently demonstrated an aptitude for. There is cause for grave concern on this point. The end result of our efforts cannot be to merely elect Big Government elephants in lieu of Big Government donkeys.

Therein is our predicament. How does the Tea Party movement affect the selection of bold new leaders and the execution of a bold new political vision, when it is not a functioning political party and has no national structure or funding? How does the Tea Party movement gain sufficient organizational structure and financial clout to substantially and permanently alter the political future of the country? This is a particularly urgent question, since 2012 is just around the corner, in the grand political scheme of things. Shortly after the November 2010 vote, candidates will begin to emerge, and platforms will begin to coalesce, for the 2012 elections. If we leave candidate selection and platform development to the Republican Party of recent vintage, we will deserve the disappointment and frustration that will be the logical outcome of such dereliction of duty.

The Tea Party movement has no choice but to infiltrate the [Republican Party] and take control.

Transforming the Republican Party

The quickest and most effective solution for this predicament is for the Tea Party movement to simply engulf and transform the Republican Party from the inside. Bizarrely, the stale carcass of the Republican Party is still the nominal standard bearer of American conservatism, in terms of the actual mechanics, funding, and structure of party politics on the right of the political spectrum. Therefore, the Republican Party is incongruously the nominal political leader of the newly energized limited-government tidal wave that it had virtually no role in cultivating.

This incongruity seems very much like the tail wagging the dog. It makes absolutely no sense.

The Tea Party movement has become the heart and soul of conservatism inside the otherwise heartless and soulless

What Is the Future of the Tea Party Movement?

GOP [Republican Party] carcass. However, despite displacing the carcass's heart and soul, the Tea Party movement has not yet gained control of the carcass's arms and legs. The newly energized activism of limited-government advocates must be first fully manifested inside the GOP, before it can be fully manifested nationally in general elections and subsequent administrations. Champions of limited government must take back the GOP, before they can take back the country.

The Tea Party movement has no choice but to infiltrate the GOP and take control of its arms and legs. If we don't do this, the arms and legs of the spiritless carcass may head in different and unpredictable directions than our conservative hearts and souls desire. The goal of our movement is to resurrect limited government beholden to the people, not to resurrect a moribund party that is beholden to itself.

We need to assert our political will inside the Republican Party, and insist that the GOP cast aside the fecklessness, ambiguity, and incompetence that caused its brand to be so brutally tarnished in the past several elections. "Throwing the bums out" should be an exercise that begins inside the GOP, before it becomes a broad nationwide electoral mission in 2012. We need to become the Republican Party's precinct delegates, its campaign volunteers and managers, its party operatives and leaders, and most importantly, its candidates. We have the energy, we have the boots on the ground, and we have the vision. We just need the will to do it.

Creating a Big-Tent Vision

This proposed palace revolt inside the GOP is not without precedent. An analogous dethroning happened during the last decade in the Democrat Party when George Soros and his Shadow Party took control of the DNC [Democratic National Committee] party machinery with billions of Soros's dollars and a phalanx of left-wing satellite organizations.

Even after the Tea Party movement figuratively assaults the ramparts of the GOP and takes control, there will still be a major void that must be addressed quickly. A critical milestone for a successful limited-government political revolution is the creation of a tenable "big tent" political vision to define it. A conservative political movement with too small of a political tent is a waste of everyone's time. We will simply be left to stand on the political sidelines shouting angry but futile epithets while the radical coalition in power continues to destroy America with ruinous spending and end-runs around the Constitution. We are not seeking the electoral consolation prize that comes with narrow, polarizing ideological purity; we are seeking victory in the form of fundamental transformation of our government.

To be very clear, we should not create an artificial and unstable big tent by compromising our principles, by collaborating with Big Government apologists, or by linking arms with appeasers and RINOs [Republicans in name only]. We will never achieve a return to limited government if we aid and abet the enemies of limited government. We have come too far with our movement just to squander our efforts by making deals with devils who will sell their souls to collectivism for the mere purpose of maintaining public office. We do not want anybody in our political tent who cannot embrace a return to limited government based on the U.S. Constitution. Period.

The key to erecting a limited-government big tent is to identify and embrace "True North" political principles that are not only inherently righteous, they resonate across a broad spectrum of the electorate. The process of doing this will necessarily require minimizing discussion of polarizing topics, and maximizing discussion of the broader and more unifying "True North" principles.

The primary "True North" principle that the conservative movement must embrace is the reestablishment of constitutionally limited government in America. Limited government reflects positively on our noble culture and tradition. It has been thoroughly proven as a successful model by the greatest country in the history of the world. Limited government is the heart and soul of the American vision. It is the most morally profound political vision in the history of mankind. It is not only right and proper as a political vision; it is the essence of the American spirit. Limited government is a framework that conservatives, libertarians, and fiscally concerned moderates and independents can rally around. Such an alliance, if fully unified, can be a powerful electoral force. This alliance will be our last stand. If such an alliance cannot successfully take back our country, then all is lost anyway.

Abandoning Conservative Litmus Tests

Such an alliance can be easily fractured, if other important but less universally agreed upon concerns are allowed to take precedence over the grander and more universally accepted principle of limited government. This is a sensitive point to make, but its very sensitivity is proof of its urgency. For example, there are many positions on social issues that conservatives hold dear. These include the right-to-life perspective on abortion, opposition to gay marriage, and support for school prayer, among many others. The "proper" positions on these issues have tended to become litmus tests for "conservative" candidates in the past.

> *We should not ... allow polarizing positions on [social] ... issues to derail [the Tea Party's] ... momentum in the political quest for limited government.*

However, in order for the limited-government movement to be successful in the 2012 elections and beyond, we have to abandon these "conservative" litmus tests. We also have to abstain from constructing planks in our political platform built around social issues. This is not to say that those who hold conservative positions on social issues should abandon them as personal commitments. Quite to the contrary, conservatives should continue to energetically advocate for their positions on social issues in families, churches, communities, schools, the media, and the marketplace.

We should not, however, allow polarizing positions on these issues to derail our momentum in the political quest for limited government. If we do not succeed in reestablishing limited government throughout America, then our positions on social issues will be steamrollered in the political forum. It is limited government or bust. If the radicals who are opposed to limited government continue to hold power in political offices, the conservative positions on social issues will be swept aside anyway. The radicals will enact adverse legislation, they will appoint antagonist judges, and they will ignore or erode the tenets of our Constitution.

Here's the brutal reality of our circumstance. The radicals in power dearly want to use the state to wage war on our conservative values. We need to gain political power to stop them. But in doing so, we will proceed as champions of limited government. As champions of limited government, we cannot propose to use political power to force our values on the rest of the nation. Therefore, the fulcrum and lever in this sticky circumstance is simply advocacy for limited government. If we pile on by emphasizing polarizing social issues, it will not gain us any friends, but it will fracture our limited government coalition.

There is only one overriding political battle right now, and there can only be one steely-eyed focus for us in the next few years. We must remove the radicals from office, and we must reestablish limited government based on the U.S. Constitution. If we don't win that battle, nothing else matters. For every social issue that we insist on polarizing the electorate with, we can automatically cross off a subset of alienated potential supporters. We gain nothing by polarizing the electorate in this manner. There is no upside. It is all downside. It will only collapse the tent of our otherwise broad coalition, tent post by bloody tent post.

A Contract with America

We need to establish a new Contract with America based solely on the principles of limited government. We need to stick with it this time. We must link arms in a broad coalition around this contract, and carry it forward through successive elections and administrations, until it becomes the mainstream of America again. For this coalition of conservatives, libertarians, and fiscally conscious moderates and independents to be successful, we need to reinforce our unity, not accentuate our divisions.

The political platform of this coalition would be built upon the "True North" principles of limited government, individual rights, individual responsibility, and the U.S. Constitution. Such a platform would:

Embrace fiscal responsibility, which means advocating a dramatic downsizing in government spending, entitlements, and involvement. It means recognizing that individuals are responsible for their lives, not the state. It means refocusing the state on protecting individual rights rather than on transferring wealth from one citizen to another. Limited government is inconsistent with entire classes of citizens being dependent on the state for sustenance.

Embrace economic growth. A growing prosperity is the only way that our society will be able to support an improved standard of living for the next generations while supporting the commitments that we have already made to the current generations. Free markets, not governments, should allocate capital and labor, price assets and resources, and choose economic winners and losers. Strong economic growth offers the potential for all people to come out ahead, not just certain groups. It promotes trade, which is the amicable and voluntary tie that binds not only citizens in America, but also countries around the world. Limited government is inconsistent with state intrusion in economic affairs.

Embrace a strong national and civil defense, but only for the purpose of protecting, with extreme prejudice, our citizens, our property, and our interests from attack by rogue nations, terrorists, and criminals. Our unalienable rights to life, liberty, and pursuing happiness are worth nothing if we cannot protect ourselves. Limited government is inconsistent with nation building and occupying foreign lands.

Insist on a judiciary that adheres to the Constitution, rather than one that seeks to unilaterally change the Constitution. The role of the judiciary is to ensure our unalienable rights are protected from the majority or an intrusive government, not dissolved by the majority or an intrusive government. Limited government is inconsistent with an activist judiciary inventing powers for the state not defined in the Constitution.

Embrace immigrants coming to America, as is our tradition, but only if they do so lawfully and can carry their own weight. Limited government is inconsistent with taking on waves of illegal immigrants dependent on the state for sustenance.

Embrace a limited-government perspective on social issues. This may run counter to the intuition of certain conservatives, but it is incongruous to demand less government in most things, while insisting that government stick its nose in moral, ethical, or religious affairs. In the context of limited government, civil libertarianism will not threaten social values held dear by conservatives or liberals. If civil liberty is properly honored, all people should be free to live their lives as they choose, according to the values that are dear to them, as long as they respect the similar rights of others. Limited government is inconsistent with the state legislating morality.

Unless the Tea Party movement takes control of the GOP and insists on a platform of limited government, not only for the purpose of winning elections but also for the purpose of actually administering the country, then the success that we have earned thus far will melt into the bitterness of lost opportunity and the gut-wrenching frustration of continuing to stand on the sidelines as the radicals and Big Government apologists from both parties ruin what's left of America.

We are passing through a life-altering fork in the road as a nation. In the 2008 elections, we headed much further and faster down the wrong fork. It is not too late (yet) to backtrack and change direction. However, if the 2010 and 2012 elections result in America continuing down the socialist fork it is currently on, then all is lost for conservatives. It's all or nothing for us, with an immediacy that can't be ignored. This is not the time for faintness of heart or half measures. Our time is now . . . or never.

The Tea Party Will Fail if It Embraces Conservative Social Issues

Jim Yardley

Jim Yardley is a retired financial controller, Vietnam veteran, writer, and blogger.

In the past week [November 29, 2010], there has been a call for the Tea Parties to introduce social issues into their "platform."

Same-sex marriage, abortion, repeal of "Don't Ask, Don't Tell," the teaching of abstinence over contraception, and numerous other agenda items of importance to social and religious conservatives have been put forth as issues that the Tea Parties should embrace. Not only should these issues be embraced, but the Tea Parties have been told that they must reconfigure their existing agenda and work toward solutions that satisfy the yearnings of these very same social and religious conservatives.

Of course, these issues are of overwhelming importance to a significant number of people. I respect that these people are sincere and truly feel that the country will be hurt beyond redemption should things continue as they are. But a significant number of vocal people do not a political majority make.

Social Issues Are No Longer Critical to Voters

The recent midterm elections were a decisive repudiation of the direction that the Democratic Party has taken the nation in the past four years, but there has been a seismic shift in

Jim Yardley, "Change Tea Party Goals?" *American Thinker*, December 1, 2010. Copyright © 2010 by Jim Yardley. All rights reserved. Reproduced by permission of American Thinker and the author.

What Is the Future of the Tea Party Movement?

what issues the majority of Americans believe to be important. What many of these religious and social conservatives fail to understand is that not one of *their* issues had any real bearing on the outcome of an election that swept sixty-plus Democrats from Congress and countless others from state and local offices. To be sure, some of the Republican winners might support some issues that social conservatives feel are important, but it was not those issues that garnered the candidate votes from independents.

This doesn't mean that the average American believes these social issues to be unimportant, but rather that issues important to social conservatives are not critical to voters at this time. According to a postelection article in the *Washington Post*:

> Social issues barely rated in this year's economy-centric midterm elections. More than six in 10 voters who cast ballots on Election Day cited the economic downturn as their top concern, according to exit polls. And this year was the first in more than a decade in which same-sex marriage did not appear on a statewide ballot.

It means that most Americans don't believe that preventing gays from serving in the military is as important as putting food on the table.

Issues important to social conservatives are not critical to voters at this time.

It means that there are more Americans who don't value school prayer as much as having a stable and reasonably compensated job.

It means that a strong majority of Americans value the idea of keeping most of what they earn over their concern about who marries whom.

These and other social issues are not unimportant. They simply didn't sway the election. They certainly do not have the unreserved support of the independent voters in this country. And today, independents are the most important component of the electorate.

No Time for Paternalism

Social and religious conservatives, like their progressive counterparts on the left, have deluded themselves. They have fallen into the trap of believing that achieving the social outcome they prefer trumps the need to build an electoral majority based on those issues that they embrace. They are trying to piggyback their agenda on top of the successes of the Tea Parties, thus (in their worldview) gaining the ability to legislate changes in society which they feel are necessary. In this, they are exactly like the liberal/progressive/Democrats [L/P/Ds]. They are displaying a willingness to legislatively coerce the majority because of their belief that they, and they alone, know what's best for all of us. The social and religious conservatives fail to recognize that it was just such an attitude that was a major cause of the disaster that hit the L/P/Ds on November 2.

Roiling the electoral waters with extraneous and highly divisive issues will only insure that the Democrats regain power.

Paternalism, from either the left or right, is not something that Americans will accept. Americans being told, directly or indirectly, that they are not competent to recognize what's best for them is viewed, quite accurately, as insulting. The Democrats and their media acolytes tried that approach and found out that at least 50 percent plus one of their constituents felt insulted ... and responded forcefully. Should social and religious conservatives follow the same path, the result will be similar, if not identical. And if Republicans think that they will gain politically by embracing and campaigning

What Is the Future of the Tea Party Movement?

wholeheartedly on the agendas of these religious and social conservatives and still garner a majority of independent voters, then they will find themselves a permanent minority party.

The country is at a crisis point, and the election of 2012—and probably the 2014 midterms as well—will be easily as critical as the 2010 midterms were. Roiling the electoral waters with extraneous and highly divisive issues (at least as evaluated by independents) will only insure that the Democrats regain power, Barack Obama is reelected, more L/P/D judicial appointments are made, more power is transferred unconstitutionally from the legislative to the executive branch of the government, and the dreams of social and religious conservatives will die a slow death.

Even worse, the dream of liberty in a free nation peopled by free people will die as well.

Tea Party Ideologues May Prevent Constructive Lawmaking by Reasonable Republicans

Steve Benen

Steve Benen is a well-known political commentator and lead blogger for Washington Monthly's Political Animal *blog.*

The effects of planned Tea Party "ambushes" in 2012.... I tend to avoid news speculating about the 2012 cycle, because it's just too far away to have any real meaning. But the *Wall Street Journal* has an important article this morning [October 7, 2010] about the elections two years from now, which I suspect will have a significant impact on policy making between now and then.

The Tea Party Threat to Reasonable Republicans

Tea Party activists, keen to build on their success toppling GOP [Republican] incumbents in primaries this year, are already targeting more Republican veterans in the 2012 election.

Sen. Olympia Snowe of Maine, one of the most liberal Republicans in Congress, already has a conservative GOP primary opponent. Sen. Orrin Hatch (R., Utah), Sen. Bob Corker (R., Tenn.) and Sen. Richard Lugar (R., Indiana) have all drawn fire from the right wing of their party.

Tea Party activists have put these and other incumbents on notice that the antiestablishment sentiment defining this year's politics will not end on Election Day 2010.

There's simply no way to say with any confidence whether any of these incumbents have anything to worry about. We

Steve Benen, "The Effects of Planned Tea Party 'Ambushes' in 2012," *Washington Monthly*, October 7, 2010. Copyright © 2010 by Steven Benen. All rights reserved. Reproduced by permission of Washington Monthly.

What Is the Future of the Tea Party Movement?

don't know whether Tea Party nonsense will fizzle over the next two years; whether their potential challengers will be seen as credible; what the state of the economy will be; etc. But after GOP primaries this year in Alaska, Utah, Delaware, Nevada, Colorado, Kentucky, and elsewhere, it's safe to assume incumbent Republicans of the sort-of-reasonable variety will have noticed the threat posed by hysterical zealots.

The Threat to Constructive Lawmaking

And in the short term, the mere *possibility* of these primary challenges will, I suspect, have a significant effect on how Congress operates, regardless of how many seats Republicans win in the midterms.

During this year's primary season, much of the talk focused on "anti-incumbent" attitudes, but that was an imprecise analysis. What we actually saw, over and over again in GOP primaries, was the willingness of the Republican base—everywhere—to punish those open to compromise and constructive policy making.

It's safe to assume incumbent Republicans of the sort-of-reasonable variety will have noticed the threat posed by hysterical [Tea Party] zealots.

[Political blogger] Jonathan Bernstein had a very good piece on this in August: "[T]hese primaries are sending a very strong message to GOP pols [politicians] about the dangers of ever allowing any space to develop between themselves and movement conservatives."

[Republican senator] Bob Bennett lost in Utah, in large part because his willingness to work with a Democrat on health care policy was deemed unacceptable to the party's base. [Republican representative] Bob Inglis was trounced in South Carolina because he expressed a willingness to work with people he disagreed with. Florida's Charlie Crist and

Pennsylvania's Arlen Specter were driven out of the party altogether because they considered it part of their responsibilities to play a constructive role in policy making. We saw [Delaware Republican representative] Mike Castle, [Alaska Republican senator] Lisa Murkowski, and others face similar problems.

It reached the point in August at which Sen. John McCain (R., Ariz.) cruised to an easy primary win after assuring Republicans he would not cooperate with anyone who doesn't agree entirely with everything he already believes.

Republican voters have sent a message to Republican lawmakers open to constructive lawmaking: Don't do it.

There can be little doubt about Tea Partiers talking about this now, more than two years before the 2012 elections: They need to instill fear before any further lawmaking. It's important, in other words, for Corker, Snowe, Hatch, and Lugar to know that if they play a constructive role in the Senate, working on public policy and considering compromise measures—in other words, if they do their jobs—their base will be watching, and that base is inclined to destroy their careers unless they vote like robotic conservative obstructionists.

Republican voters have sent a message to Republican lawmakers open to constructive lawmaking: Don't do it. Party activists don't want responsible leaders who'll try to solve problems; they want hard-right ideologues. No exceptions.

The Tea Party Could Produce Political Chaos

Steven J. Gulitti

Steven J. Gulitti is a writer from New York City and author of Steven J. Gulitti's Blog.

In the event of a Republican takeover of one or both houses of Congress on November 2nd [2010], it won't be long before the Tea Party movement and the G.O.P. [Republican Party] will be involved in one or more train wrecks, some of which could be pretty dramatic. These train wrecks will arise from fundamental differences in philosophy and will occur over a period of time that could begin sooner rather than later. Upending Republican establishmentarians during primaries was relatively easy; winning general elections where competitive ideas are at issue could be a bit harder. Governing will be much harder still, particularly when you take into account the differences between Tea Party rhetoric and American political reality.

The Institutional Nature of Congress

The first obstacle newly elected members of the movement will face is the institutional nature of Congress. Tea Party freshmen in both the House and Senate will be at the bottom of congressional seniority lists and thus not immediately in line for leadership roles as committee chairpersons. Thus they will be in the position of having to sell their policy proposals to the existing leadership. That leadership may be more amenable to the ideas of the newcomers given the fact that several veteran Republican lawmakers are no longer around thanks to the Tea Party. Conversely the G.O.P. leaders may let Congress

Steven J. Gulitti, "An Impending and Inevitable Train Wreck," *Open Salon*, October 31, 2010. www.open.salon.com. Copyright © 2010 by Steven J. Gulitti. All rights reserved. Reproduced by permission of the author.

work the way it always has thereby attenuating the influence of the Tea Party. In the Senate in particular the likely Republican winners are veteran politicians who will come to the office with considerable experience. According to political observer David Herszenhorn: "Insurgent challengers may be grabbing all the headlines in midterm elections this year, but most of the Republicans who are best positioned to snap up Senate seats currently held by Democrats are veteran politicians—and most of them have already served in Congress. Based on their experience, the 2010 class of Senate Republican freshman could well prove to be relatively pragmatic and wise to the ways of legislative deal making—almost certainly more so than the Tea Party–backed firebrands like Sharron Angle in Nevada and Rand Paul in Kentucky, who have built their campaigns around ideological demands and an end to business as usual." In all of the discussions surrounding this election, few have pointed out the difference between those candidates who come out of, or are closely aligned with, the Tea Party movement and those who have received the movement's support solely because of their Republican affiliation. This second group will not necessarily move in lockstep with the hard-core ideologues of the Tea Party seeing as they are not beholden to the movement in any meaningful way. Therein lay the seeds of intra-party conflict and controversy.

Facing Reality on Spending Cuts

The next challenge facing newly elected members of the Tea Party movement will be the reconciliation of their penchant for spending cuts and ending earmarks versus what can be achieved in the realm of the possible. These desires will butt up against the fact that cutting government spending during a severe economic downturn could only make things worse and many Republicans favor an ending of the G.O.P.'s moratorium on the use of earmarks. There's a reason that the G.O.P's leadership has been mum on the political talk show circuit when

What Is the Future of the Tea Party Movement?

it comes to detailing the particulars of spending cuts and the reason is that they don't have a viable plan. Even as late in the game as this morning, [Mississippi governor] Haley Barbour, appearing on [the TV Show] *Meet the Press* was unable or unwilling to fill in the blanks when asked how a Republican-controlled Congress will reduce the size of government. [NBC News anchor] Tom Brokaw, appearing on this same show pointed out that many Republican candidates have made rash promises on the campaign trail that can't be kept or will be nearly impossible to keep given the current political situation. Again we see the future of conflict as already being baked into the cake, so to speak.

There is little reason to believe that the Republican rhetoric of the campaign trail will carry over to policies that actually achieve what that rhetoric has promised.

I read "A Pledge to America" and it is full of general statements regarding spending cuts, but for the scope of its discussion, it lays out few policy specifics. The "Pledge" is equal parts indictment, rallying cry and act of contrition, but what it isn't is a blueprint for reducing government. I can't help but wonder why the G.O.P. trotted out the "Pledge" when they have Congressman Paul Ryan's (R-WI) "A Roadmap for America's Future," which is a well-reasoned analysis full of specific proposed cuts. Again to Herszenhorn: "while polls show that the Republicans' message is succeeding politically, Republican candidates and party leaders are offering few specifics about how they would tackle the nation's $13.7 trillion debt, and budget analysts said the party was glossing over the difficulty of carrying out its ideas, especially when sharp spending cuts could impede an already weak economic recovery . . . (both) parties share blame for the current fiscal situation, but federal budget statistics show that Republican policies over the last decade, and the cost of the two wars, added far more to the deficit than initiatives approved by the Democratic Congress since 2006.... Calculations by the nonpartisan Congressional Budget Office and other independent fiscal experts show that the $1.1 trillion cost over the next 10 years of the Medicare prescription drug program, which the Republican-controlled Congress adopted in 2003, by itself would add more to the deficit than the combined costs of the bailout, the stimulus and the health care law." Moreover, most Republicans are calling for the permanent extension of all [George W.] Bush-era tax cuts and that would add $700 billion more to the deficit over the next 10 years.

The "Pledge" has come in for scathing criticism on the right as well as the left. Janet Hook and Naftali Bendavid of the *Wall Street Journal* made the following observations: "The new policy manifesto released by House Republicans Thursday is laced with ideas and rhetoric designed to appeal to the surging tea-party movement. But it left some conservatives disappointed with its omissions and complaining that the plan had limited sweep.... Yet the new agenda was silent on some of the most sought-after goals on the tea-party wish list, such as a balanced budget constitutional amendment and a ban on special-interest appropriations called earmarks." Many conservatives look to what is now happening in the United Kingdom as a model of inspiration for cutbacks here. But that program involves a significant reduction in defense spending; something that would have to be included here as well as those outlays constitutes 58% of discretionary federal spending. With a large portion of federal spending being committed to Social Security, Medicare, Medicaid and paying off interest on Treasury bonds, the amount of money subject to discretionary spending reduction is only one-third of all outlays. There is a growing minority within the G.O.P. on Capitol Hill who are making the case that the projected debt is too big to handle through spending cuts alone. According to Saxby Chambliss (R-GA): "Everything has got to be on the table for discussion.... There are a lot of things people are going to have to be educated about, on the spending side as well as the revenue side. They're thinking we can come in and eliminate earmarks and everybody's going to be happy on the spending side. Gee, that just scratches the surface." Is Senator Chambliss tacitly acknowledging that tax cuts will have to expire or even that tax increases may be needed to deal with the deficit? The "Pledge" is notoriously silent on the subject of earmarks and seeing as they are a major source of spending, this is sure to give rise to a rift within the new Republican caucus on Capitol Hill. It doesn't take a soothsayer or a professional handicapper to see that the G.O.P. and the Tea Party movement are on a collision course with regard to spending and the practical ability to rein in that spending given the current economic situation and the present composition of federal government outlays. Thus there is little reason to believe that the Republican rhetoric of the campaign trail will carry over to policies that actually achieve what that rhetoric has promised. Therein lies the root of yet another G.O.P.–Tea Party collision.

The Tea Party movement will continue to run up against the fact that many of its essential beliefs are divorced from reality and therein lay the seeds of train wrecks to come.

The Effect of Wealthy Special Interests on Tea Party Issues

Newly elected Tea Party movement lawmakers may find themselves running into some strong headwinds in the form of those special interests that have invested heavily in this election on behalf of conservative causes. While it is now likely that in the final analysis Democrats may end up spending more money than their opposition, there is an unprecedented amount of money flowing to the Republican side from outside sources as a result of the *Citizens United* ruling [referring to the 2010 Supreme Court decision in *Citizens United v. Federal Election Commission*]. According to OpenSecrets.org the 2010 midterms have seen a whooping 186.7 million dollars flowing into Republican coffers vice 88.6 million for the Democrats. Likewise an article on the U.S. Chamber of Commerce and business donations shows the tide running against the Democrats among these groups at a rate of almost two to one. Ostensibly one would say what difference does it make where all this money is coming from if the Democrats are actually spending more? But within the confines of this argument, what matters is that this tidal wave of money spent by outside interests is being spent for a reason, to influence the election's outcome and thereafter to buy influence with the winners. Washington lobbyists are already courting the potential new congressional chairmen and in the process could effectively be outmaneuvering the Tea Party activists in the game of power and influence. Thus the many questions that beg to be asked: Won't all of this money muscle out the grassroots crowd and how will the Tea Party activists compete for attention with the lobbyists who are already prowling the halls of Congress and the bars and restaurants of downtown Washington? Is the movement about to get mugged on K Street? Are the rank-and-file Tea Party patriots in the process of "taking their country back" just to have it taken away in turn by the wealthy interests who have spent all of this money to influence the outcome of the 2010 elections? Surely this money was not spent because it was burning a hole in someone's pocket. Does anyone believe that these special interests were in the mood to do the activists a favor on November 2nd? Will the rank-and-file Tea Partier unwittingly deliver "his country" as a gift to a new class of plutocrats that will have no use for him except for his vote during the next election cycle and his attendance at rallies? Don't look now but we may be about to witness the greatest political hustle since the evangelicals came out in force for George W. Bush only to get nothing of substance in the bargain.

Train Wrecks to Come

Finally, the Tea Party movement will continue to run up against the fact that many of its essential beliefs are divorced from reality and therein lay the seeds of train wrecks to come. First and foremost is one of its core ideas, that Americans are overtaxed. The fact is that taxes are as low as they have been in sixty years; lower than they were when Ronald Reagan was president. As Senator Chambliss implied above, increased taxes may be inevitable if people are serious about reducing the deficit. The Tea Party waxes nostalgic for the Reagan era, yet unemployment was higher when the "Gipper" went into his first midterm election than it is now and his approval rating was roughly the same as Obama's. The movement preaches fiscal restraint while refusing to consider reductions in defense spending where wasteful spending is well documented and widespread. This will lead to calls for a reduction in social programs during the worst economic downturn since the 1930s and that will only create resistance on the left and reluctance on the part of practical Republican officeholders on the right. The Tea Partiers clamor, "keep your hands off my Medicare" but underplay how to rein in the program's cost increases. They rail against TARP [Troubled Asset Relief Program], blaming Obama for its inception all the while ignoring the fact that many of the very Republicans running for reelection are the ones who originally put the bailout in place. How will they address the fact that TARP's costs will be less than originally anticipated? Even conservative observer Ross Douthat admits that for all its shortcomings TARP was a necessary evil at the time of its inception. On the issue of repealing health care reform there is now no clear consensus to do so, according to the latest CBS poll, yet repeal is a major Tea Party goal.

The continued Tea Party fixation with Obama as a socialist, fascist or both at the same time reveals a lack of understanding of what actually comprises these two somewhat similar yet fundamentally different schools of political thought. If it's not that, then what else could it be other than a deliberate attempt to misinform the public for partisan ends. It goes without saying that this is something that can only contribute to further gridlock. This fact stands in direct contrast to what the public rants. The latest polling by both Bloomberg and the *New York Times*/CBS News reveals an electorate that wants compromise not confrontation. Yet with the arrival of Tea Party–backed lawmakers the stage is now set for a political environment more favorable to confrontation than to compromise. Attempts to fix the blame on President Obama for the current economic situation are likely to fail as well as "nearly 60 percent of Americans were optimistic about Mr. Obama's next two years in office and nearly 70 percent said the economic slump is temporary. Half said the economy was where they expected it would be at this point, and less than 10 percent blamed the current administration for the state of the economy, leaving the onus on former president George W. Bush and Wall Street." In the final analysis, the 2010 election is shaping up to be something of an anomaly. On the one hand you have widespread voter dissatisfaction with the status quo while at the same time the party likely to gain seats has a favorability rating below the party that will be turned out of office. Thus for the Republicans this victory will be a political windfall rather than an endorsement of the party and its platform. The G.O.P. will find itself in an inopportune marriage of convenience with the Tea Party movement which in the long haul may turn out to the G.O.P.'s detriment as the public grows weary of the gridlock and political train wrecks that are sure to come. Rather than being on the cusp of a Republican revival or a "return to our core values" we are more likely on the verge of an environment of political chaos which is just

What Is the Future of the Tea Party Movement?

what we don't need at this point in time and that chaos may well come back to haunt the Republican Party and hobble its chances in the 2012 election and beyond. Ladies and Gentlemen, fasten your seat belts.

Organizations to Contact

The editors have compiled the following list of organizations concerned with the issues debated in this book. The descriptions are derived from materials provided by the organizations. All have publications or information available for interested readers. The list was compiled on the date of publication of the present volume; names, addresses, phone and fax numbers, and e-mail and Internet addresses may change. Be aware that many organizations take several weeks or longer to respond to inquiries, so allow as much time as possible.

Cato Institute
1000 Massachusetts Avenue NW
Washington, DC 20001-5403
(202) 842-0200 • fax: (202) 842-3490
website: www.cato.org

The Cato Institute is a libertarian public policy research foundation that promotes public policies based on the principles of limited government, free markets, individual liberty, and peace. The group publishes a variety of publications including books, monographs, briefing papers, and shorter studies, as well as the quarterly magazine *Regulation* and a bimonthly newsletter, *Cato Policy Report*. A search of the Cato website for Tea Party reveals numerous relevant entries including "Tea Partiers Shouldn't Date the GOP" and "The Not-So-White Tea Party."

Center for American Progress (CAP)
1333 H Street NW, 10th Floor, Washington, DC 20005
(202) 682-1611 • fax: (202) 682-1867
website: www.americanprogress.org

The Center for American Progress (CAP) is a progressive think tank that works on twenty-first-century challenges such as energy, national security, economic growth and opportunity, immigration, education, and health care. CAP develops new policy ideas, critiques the policies that stem from conservative values, and challenges the media to cover the issues that truly matter. The group also produces numerous articles and policy papers, and sponsors *Think Progress*, a blog that advances progressive ideas and policies. Recent publications on the topic of the Tea Party include "Public Opinion Snapshot: The Tea Party vs. the Public" and "Think Again: Tea Party/Fox Party."

Heritage Foundation
214 Massachusetts Avenue NE, Washington, DC 20002-4999
(202) 546-4400
e-mail: info@heritage.org
website: www.heritage.org

The Heritage Foundation is a conservative think tank that seeks to formulate and promote conservative public policies based on the principles of free enterprise, limited government, individual freedom, traditional American values, and a strong national defense. The foundation supports Tea Party activities, and a search of its website produces a long list of articles about the Tea Party including "New Progressive America or Tea Party Nation?" and "Tea Party Must Tackle Defense Issues."

Institute for Policy Studies (IPS)
1112 Sixteenth Street NW, Suite 600, Washington, DC 20036
(202) 234-9382
e-mail: info@ips-dc.org
website: www.ips-dc.org

The Institute for Policy Studies (IPS) is a multi-issue progressive think tank that has served as a policy and research resource for social justice movements for more than four decades—from the antiwar and civil rights movements in the 1960s to the peace and global justice movements of the last decade. Today the institute's work is organized into more than a dozen projects, but these projects collaborate strategically to pursue three overarching policy goals: peace, justice, and environment. Examples of publications relating to the Tea Party include "A Progressive-Tea Party Foreign Policy Coalition?" and "Don't Hold Your Breath: Tea Party at the Pentagon?"

Rand Paul for US Senate
PO Box 101, Bowling Green, KY 42101
(866) 232-9747
website: www.randpaul2010.com

Rand Paul for US Senate is the website of Rand Paul, who in the midterm elections of 2010 was elected senator from Kentucky after openly declaring his support for the Tea Party. He describes himself as a constitutional conservative and a libertarian, and he is viewed by many political observers as a leader of the Tea Party movement. His website describes his positions on various issues and contains press releases, news, and articles. An example is "Senator-Elect Rand Paul Statement on Obamacare Ruling."

Tea Party Patriots Inc.
e-mail: mark@teapartypatriots.org
website: www.teapartypatriots.org

Tea Party Patriots Inc., one of the most prominent Tea Party groups, operates as a social welfare organization organized under section 501(c)(4) of the Internal Revenue Code. It describes itself as a nonpartisan, nonprofit grassroots organization dedicated to furthering the common good and general welfare of the people of the United States by educating the public and promoting the principles of fiscal responsibility, constitutionally limited government, and free markets. The group's website is a good source of information for Tea Party views on pending legislation and other matters. An example is "Today Is a Win for the U.S. Constitution," an article praising a federal court ruling that held President Barack Obama's health care reforms to be unconstitutional.

Bibliography

Books

Dick Armey and Matt Kibbe	*Give Us Liberty: A Tea Party Manifesto*. New York: HarperCollins, 2011.
B. Leland Baker	*Tea Party Revival: The Conscience of a Conservative Reborn: The Tea Party Revolt Against Unconstrained Spending and Growth of the Federal Government*. Denver, CO: Outskirts Press, 2009.
Bruce Bexley	*The Tea Party Movement: Why It Started, What It's About, and How You Can Get Involved*. Seattle, WA: CreateSpace, 2009.
Will Bunch	*The Backlash: Right-Wing Radicals, High-Def Hucksters, and Paranoid Politics in the Age of Obama*. New York: HarperCollins, 2010.
Sharon Cooper and Chuck Asay	*Taxpayers' Tea Party: How to Become Politically Active—and Why*. Riverdale, NY: Baen, 2010.
William Davis Eaton	*The Liberal Betrayal of America and the Firestorm Tea Party Response: How the Student Riots of the Sixties Generated a Civil War to Destroy a Great Nation*. Oakland, OR: Elderberry Press, 2010.

Joseph Farah	*The Tea Party Manifesto: A Vision of an American Rebirth.* Washington, DC: WND Books, 2010.
Michael Graham	*That's No Angry Mob, That's My Mom: Team Obama's Assault on Tea-Party, Talk-Radio Americans.* Washington, DC: Regnery Pub., 2010.
Charly Gullett	*Official Tea Party Handbook: A Tactical Playbook for Tea Party Patriots.* Prescott, AR: Warfield Press, 2009.
Erin McHugh	*Coffee, Tea, or Kool-Aid: Which Party Politics Are You Swallowing?* New York: Abrams Image, 2010.
Brent Morehouse	*Tea Party: The Awakening.* Corona Del Mar, CA: New Patriot Publishing, 2010.
John M. O'Hara	*A New American Tea Party: The Counterrevolution Against Bailouts, Handouts, Reckless Spending, and More Taxes.* Hoboken, NJ: Wiley, 2010.
Bill Press	*Toxic Talk: How the Radical Right Has Poisoned America's Airwaves.* New York: Thomas Dunne Books, 2010.
Scott Rasmussen and Doug Schoen	*Mad as Hell: How the Tea Party Movement Is Fundamentally Remaking Our Two-Party System.* New York: HarperCollins, 2010.

Robin Rohr	*Tea Party: American Revolution 2.0: Silent Majority, Silent No More.* Seattle, WA: CreateSpace, 2010.
Kate Zernike	*Boiling Mad: Inside Tea Party America.* New York: Times Books/Henry Holt and Co., 2010.

Periodicals and Internet Sources

Naftali Bendavid	"Tea-Party Activists Complicate Republican Comeback Strategy," *Wall Street Journal*, October 16, 2010.
Chip Berlet	"Taking Tea Partiers Seriously," *Progressive*, February 2010.
Wayne Besen	"Fundamentalists and Tea Party May Destroy the Earth," *Truth Wins Out*, October 22, 2010. www.truthwinsout.org.
Arian Campo-Flores	"Are Tea Partiers Racist?" *Newsweek*, April 26, 2010.
Climate Progress	"Why the Victory of the Tea Party Extremists (Backed by Big Oil) over the Slightly Less Extreme GOP Establishment (Also Backed by Big Oil) Is Good for Progressives, but Bad for Climate and Clean Energy," September 15, 2010. http://climateprogress.org.
Tom Cohen	"Tea Party: Return to Basics or Divisive Force on Right?" *CNN*, September 27, 2010. www.cnn.com.

Dave Cook	"Tea Party Splits GOP in Thirds, Says Republican Strategist," *Christian Science Monitor*, November 4, 2010.
Elizabeth Dickinson and Joshua E. Keating	"The Horror, the Horror ... and the Pity: How the International Media Is Covering the Tea Party," *Foreign Policy*, October 26, 2010. www.foreignpolicy.com.
Thomas L. Friedman	"Third Party Rising," *New York Times*, October 2, 2010.
Joshua Green	"The Tea Party's Brain," *Atlantic*, November 2010.
Mark Halperin	"How the Tea Party May Hurt GOP Senate Prospects," *Time*, July 12, 2010.
John B. Judis	"Lost Generation: The Election That Made Us Japan," *New Republic*, November 10, 2010.
Jonathan Martin and Ben Smith	"The Tea Party's Exaggerated Importance," *Politico*, April 22, 2010. www.politico.com.
John Prince and Arjun Mody	"Crashing the Party," *Harvard Political Review*, October 26, 2010. http://hpronline.org.
Jeffrey Rosen	"Radical Constitutionalism," *New York Times Magazine*, November 26, 2010.
Mark Sappenfield	"Rand Paul and the Limits of the 'Tea Party' Revolution," *Christian Science Monitor*, May 23, 2010.

Kyle Trygstad	"Gallup: Tea Party: Rebranding Republicanism," *Real Clear Politics*, July 2, 2010. http://realclearpolitics.blogs.time.com.
Wall Street Journal	"The Tea Party and the GOP," September 8, 2010.
Justin Wolfers	"Did the Tea Party Help or Hurt the Republicans?" *New York Times*, November 3, 2010.
Kate Zernike	"Republicans Get a Partner, but Who Will Lead?" *New York Times*, September 15, 2010.

Index

A

ACORN (Association of Community Organizations for Reform Now), 106, 146
Afghanistan war, 18
African Americans
    Tea Party absence of racism, 80–83
    Tea Party activism by, 55, 81–83
Alaska primary election, 161
Alexandrovna, Larisa, 47–49
Alinsky, Saul, 58
American Israel Political Affairs Committee (AIPAC), 122
American Recovery and Reinvestment Act (2009), 26–27, 111
Americans for Prosperity (corporate front group), 20, 104
Angle, Sharron
    anti-Social Security, anti-Medicare stance, 101
    endorsement of Joe Arpaio, 118
    loss to Harry Reid, 24, 29, 33
    Palin's aid to, 128
    symbolism of participation, 132–133
Anti-Semitic attacks, 84, 85
Arizona
    illegal alien problems, 35
    midterm victory of McCain, 162
Arkansas National Guard troopers, 87
Armey, Dick, 35, 101, 118

Arpaio, Joe, 118
Association of Community Organizations for Reform Now (ACORN), 106, 146
Atlanta (GA) tea party groups, 132
Atwater, Lee, 67–68
Authoritarian worldview, 40–41
Authoritarianism & Polarization in American Politics (Hetherington and Weiler), 40
Ayotte, Kelly, 32

B

Bachmann, Michelle, 32, 36, 97, 141, 143
Baker, Ross, 52–53
Balanced federal budget, 19, 97–98, 105, 107, 125, 131–132, 135
Bank bailouts, 19, 68–69, 135
Banking, Housing, Urban Affairs Committee (Senate), 34
Barbour, Haley, 100, 165
Barstow, David, 68
Bauer, Karl, 84
Beck, Glenn, 44, 45, 83, 113, 121
Benen, Steve, 160–162
Bennett, Bob, 29, 45
Berger, Richard, 84
Berkowitz, Bill, 57–61
Berland, Penn Schoen, 50
The Big Black Lie: How I Learned the Truth About the Democrat Party (Jackson), 81
Birther movement, 47, 64, 96

Index

Black Caucus, Congressional, 56, 81
Blackmon, Douglas A., 130–133
Blood and Politics: The History of White Nationalism from the Margins to the Mainstream (Zeskind), 60
Blow, Charles, 80
Boehner, John A., 141
Boiling Mad: Inside Tea Party America (Zernike), 117
Borelli, Deneen, 81
Boston Tea Party, 18, 31–32, 48–49, 70
Boxer, Barbara, 101
Brady, Kevin, 123
Brokaw, Tom, 165
Brown, Scott, 23
Bryant, C. L., 81–82
Buchanan, Pat, 60
Buffett, Warren, 20
Burghart, Devin, 59–60
Bush, George H. W., 52
Bush, George W. (and administration)
    bank bailouts, 19, 68–69, 135
    Castle's call for impeachment, 123
    inactivity of Tea Party, 78
    initiation of TARP program, 19
    Obama's policy similarities, 79
    post-era conservatism, 139
    tax cuts, 39
    vilification of, while in office, 64

C

California
    balanced budget attempts, 107
    House Rules Committee representation, 124
    illegal alien problems, 35
    Tea Party candidates, 124
Campaign for America's Future think tank, 134
Cantor, Eric, 101, 122
Cap and trade environmental policy, 27, 55, 96, 105, 106–107
Carter, Graydon, 88
Carter, Jimmy, 99
Castle, Mike, 123–124
CBS/*New York Times* poll, 72
Cedar Hills Baptist Church (Louisiana), 82
Cesca, Bob, 66–71
Chambliss, Saxby, 166–167
Chapman-Smith, Robert, 77–79
Christian Right activism, 60–61, 75
Citizen opposition to Tea Party, 50–53
Citizens United v. Federal Election Commission (Supreme Court ruling), 168
Civil rights movement (U.S.), 38
Cleaver, Emanuel, 87
Clinton, Bill, 52, 88, 113
Clyburn, James, 81
CNN *Capital Gang*, 123
CNN report, 94, 123
Committee on Environment and Public Works, 101
Congress
    American Recovery and Reinvestment Act, 26–27
    "don't ask, don't tell" policy rejection, 55
    growing Tea Party influence, 130–132

healthcare legislation, 55, 57, 92
institutional nature of, 163–164
TARP legislation, 3, 19, 68, 169
Congressional Black Caucus, 56, 81
Conservative Political Action Conference (CPAC), 112–114
Contract from America (Tea Party), 96, 105–111
- anti-health care stance, 109–110
- demand for a balanced budget, 107–108
- earmark moratorium, 111
- ending runaway government spending, 109
- fiscal responsibility, limited government, 108
- fundamental tax reform enactment, 108
- pass on "all-of-the-above" energy policy, 110
- protection of the Constitution, 106
- rejection of cap and trade, 106–107
- stopping tax hikes, 111

Contract with America, 145, 153–155
Conway, Jack, 132
Coons, Chris, 124
Corker, Bob, 160
Corporate funding of the Tea Party
- Americans for Prosperity, 20, 104
- benefits to candidates, 43, 45–46
- candidate belief in corporations, 35–36
- conflicts with sponsors, 25
- FreedomWorks, 43, 104
- funding, exploitation of candidates, 47–49
- possible betrayal of politicians, 134–137
- Tea Party opposition, 44

Coulter, Ann, 113–115
Crist, Charlie, 24, 130

D

Daily Show (Jon Stewart), 98
Dean, Howard, 78
Delaware primary election, 161
DeMint, Jim, 97, 131
Democratic National Committee (DNC), 78, 149
Democratic Party
- losses in midterm elections, 45
- misunderstanding of Tea Party, 26
- opposition to Tea Party, 52
- post-1972 election-style endorsements, 125
- support for Third Party, 50
- Tea Party commonalities, 120
- Tea Party distrust of, 27

Demographics of Tea Party members, 75
Dionne, E. J., 75
Dodd, Christopher, 34
"Don't ask, don't tell" gay military policy, 55, 156–157
Douthat, Ross, 138
Dreier, David, 124
Duke, David, 87

Index

E

Election primaries (for 2012 election), 128–129
"Election Projections Fuel Tea Party Fervor" (CNN report), 94
Erickson, Erick, 113
Evangelical Christians, 75, 81

F

Farah, Joseph, 47
Federal Reserve (the Fed), 91
Feingold, Russ, 43–44
Food safety bill passage, 43
Foreign oil addiction, 136
Foreign policy
    Bush-era doctrines, 79
    conservative vs. progressive paradigm, 103
    Rand Paul/Libertarian viewpoint, 116
    relationship of Tea Party, 92
    Tea Party vs. Republican Party, 117–122
    Tea Party's lack of, 117–118
    viewpoint of Ann Coulter, 113, 115
Foreign Policy magazine, 120
Fortuyn, Pim, 139–140
Founding Fathers (of the US), 49
Fox, J. Wesley, 26–30
Fox News Channel, 67
Frank, Barney, 120
Free trade, Tea Party suspicion about, 119
FreedomWorks (corporate front group), 43, 104

G

Gallup poll, 95
Gates, Bill, 20
Gay people/gay rights, 38, 40, 47, 80, 124–125, 151
    See also LGBT rights movement
German Reich anti-Jewish violence (1938), 84
Gewen, Barry, 117–122
Gilmore, Ellen, 132
Gingrich, Newt, 101
Globalization, Tea Party suspicion about, 119
Goldhagen, Daniel Jonah, 86
Goldstein, Aaron, 80–83
Gore, Al, 52
Graham, Lindsey, 97
Grayson, Trey, 29
Great Depression, 19
Greenwald, Glenn, 112–116
Guantanamo Bay detention camp, 115
Gulitti, Steven J., 163–171

H

Haley, Nikki, 24
Hastert, Dennis, 29
Hatch, Orrin, 45, 160
Hawkins, John, 59
Health care legislation (ObamaCare), 55, 57, 92, 109
Hetherington, Marc J., 40
Heydrich, Reinhard, 84
Hill 2010 Midterm Election Poll, 50, 51
Hilton, Paris, 87

Hitler's Willing Executioners: Ordinary Germans and the Holocaust (Goldhagen), 86
Holland, Keating, 95
Homeowner Affordability and Stability Plan (Obama), 31
Hoover, Herbert, 100
Horton, Willie, 67
Hot Tea Radio program (Glenn Beck), 83
House of Representatives
    Chapman-Smith's service, 77
    midterm election protests, 23
    Rand Paul's votes against all tax bills, 92
    responsiveness to mood of U.S., 33
    Tea Party members, 24
    Tim Scott's election to, 55
Huckabee, Mike, 63, 98, 114
Huffington Post, 87
Hultgren, Randy, 29

I

Immigration reforms
    amnesty for illegals, 55
    Tancredo's anti-immigrant speech, 41
    Tea Party problems with, 34–35, 59, 104
    Tea Party vs. Republican beliefs, 118–119
Indianapolis Colts, 82–83
Inglis, Bob, 29
Inhofe, James M., 101
Institute for Research & Education on Human Rights, 59–60
Insurrection Resurrection: A Novel of Political and Religious Satire (Keena), 145

Iranian Green movement, 38, 40
Iraq war, 18, 104
Irving, David, 87
"Is the Tea Party or Conservs the Modern Day Klan?" *(Daily Kos)*, 80

J

Jackson, Jesse, 87
Jackson, Kevin, 81–82
Jewish community, violence against (1938), 84, 85
Johnson, Dave, 134–137
Johnson, Ron, 43–44
Johnson, Sam, 123

K

Keena, James R., 145–155
Kendall, Mary Claire, 31–33
Kennedy, Edward "Ted," 23
Khimm, Suzy, 45
King, Colbert, 81, 86–87
Kirk, Mark, 44
Know Nothing movement, 34, 35
Koch, David and Charles, 20, 136
Krugman, Paul, 88–89, 86

L

Latinos
    perceptions about Tea Party, 96
    support of Tea Party, 59
    UW poll information, 72
Lee, Mike, 101
Legislation
    cap and trade policy, 27, 55, 96, 105, 106–107
    climate cap-and-trade, 55

Index

food safety bill passage, 43
health care (ObamaCare), 55, 57, 92, 109
questionable Tea Party impact, 24–25
Tea Party weakness, 43–45
Troubled Asset Relief Program, 3, 19, 68, 169
Levitz, Jennifer, 130–133
Lewis, John, 81, 87
LGBT (lesbian, gay, bisexual, transgender) rights movement, 38
Liberal-Democratic Party (Russia), 139
Libertarian Party, 18, 20, 52
  acceptance sought by, 115–116
  anti-tax stance, 60
  maximization of individual rights, 191
  Republicans vs., 92, 112–116
  Tea Party adoption of policies of, 18–19, 80
  Tea Party stance against, 104
  See also Americans for Prosperity; FreedomWorks; Paul, Ron
Limbaugh, Rush, 67, 123, 138
List in the Netherlands (political movement), 139
Los Angeles Times, 99
Losing the Race: Self-Sabotage in Black America (McWhorter), 74
Lowden, Sue, 29
Lugar, Richard, 160
Lupica, Mike, 86

M

Mad as Hell: How the Tea Party Movement Is Fundamentally Remaking Our Two-Party System (Schoen & Rasmussen), 119
Martin, Jenny Beth, 97–98, 130, 131
McCain, John, 94, 95, 120, 162
McCain-Palin rally (2008 presidential race), 94
McKinnon, Mark, 51, 53
McManus, Doyle, 141–144
McWhirter, Cameron, 130–133
McWhorter, John, 74
Medicare, 21, 101, 119
Meek, Kendrick, 130
Meloy, Joe, 123
Mencimer, Stephanie, 43–46
Midterm elections (2010)
  anger at losses, 32–33
  Democratic Party losses, 45
  Hill 2010 Midterm Election Poll, 50, 51
  loss by O'Donnell, 130
  onset of Tea Party activism, 130–133
  Tea Party victories, 19–20, 23–24, 31–33
  victory of Rubio, 24, 32–33, 94, 130
Military
  budgetary/spending concerns, 92, 109, 122, 127–128, 136
  "don't ask, don't tell" gay policy, 55, 156–157
  global U.S. presence, 120
  torture policies, 115
Miller, Joe, 101, 133
Miller, Sean J., 50–53
Moderate Republicans, threats of Tea Party, 45–46
Mother Jones magazine, 138

185

MoveOn (progressive political group), 44, 146
Moynihan, Michael C., 84–89

N

Nader, Ralph, 52
NAFTA (North American Free Trade Agreement), 134
National Review, 113
National Security State, 113
National Tea Party Convention, 39–40, 47
National Tea Party Federation, 143
Neocons (neoconservatives), 115–116, 121, 139
Netanyahu, Benjamin, 121
Nevada primary election, 161
New Hampshire election primary, 129, 138
New Junkie Post (web-based news site), 103
New Mexico, illegal alien problems, 35
New Orleans Saints, 82
"New People" characterization, of Tea Party, 124
New York Daily News, 86
New York Times article, 80
"NewsHour with Jim Lehrer" (PBS), 123
NPR (National Public Radio), 48

O

Obama, Barack
  alleged radicalism, 99
  anti-Obama demonstrations, 57, 59
  bank bailouts, 19, 68–69, 135
  Birther movement vs., 47, 64, 96
  denigration by Limbaugh, 67
  health care legislation, 55, 57, 92, 109
  Homeowner Affordability and Stability Plan, 31
  Internet election campaign, 79
  Palin's possible run against, 128–129
  permission for coastal offshore drilling, 110
  possible foreign war withdrawals, 122
  Quinn's denigration of, 70–71
  similarities with Bush, 79
  South Korea free trade pact, 119
  Tea Partiers' disgust with, 27, 62–65, 69–70
  2008 presidential victory, 19
  2012 reelection campaign, 125
O'Donnell, Christine, 33, 138
  absence of credibility, 24, 32
  Limbaugh's endorsement of, 123
  midterm election loss, 130
  odd beliefs of, 100
  Palin's endorsement of, 123, 128
  primary upset, 124
  symbolism of participation, 133
Olson, Ole Ole, 103–111
Organizing for America organization, 146
O'Rourke, P.J., 118
Outsourcing, 134–135

P

Paladino, Carl, 130, 139
Palin, Sarah
    alignment with Tea Party, 20, 32
    as face of Tea Party, 127
    Haley endorsement from, 24
    keynote convention speech, 39–40, 47, 115, 127–128
    O'Donnell endorsement from, 123
    possible run against Obama, 128–129
    Rand Paul endorsement from, 113
    Rubio endorsement from, 128
    Scott endorsement from, 55
    Tea Party rally appearances, 83
    vs. Ron Paul, 121–122
    winning candidates aided by, 128
Parker, Christopher, 73
Paul, Rand (son of Ron Paul)
    anti-Federal Reserve stance, 91
    call for end to foreign wars, 120
    departmental elimination proposals, 100
    election to US Senate, 20, 29, 62–63, 91, 130
    Palin's aid to, 128
    prediction of Tea Party landslide victories, 132
    self-identification to Tea Party, 24
    "taking back government" rhetoric, 62–63
    The Tea Party Goes to Washington, 93
    votes against all tax bills, 92
Paul, Ron
    anti-tax stance, 60
    call for end to foreign wars, 120
    campaign events, 104
    holding of first Tea Party protest, 78
    Internet election campaign, 79
    invocation of Boston Tea Party imagery, 78
    2008 presidential candidate, 18, 52, 78
Pawlenty, Tim, 97
Penn, Mark, 50
Perot, Ross, 35, 52, 139–140
    See also United We Stand America
Perspectives website, 94–98
Phillips, Judson, 53
"Pledge to America" (Republican Party), 96
Podhoretz, John, 122
Political action committees (PACs), 29–30
Polls
    CBS/*New York Times*, 72
    Economist, 109
    healthcare reform legislation, 58
    Hill 2010 Midterm Election Poll, 50, 51
    Quinnipiac University, 95
    Times/CBS poll, 74–75
    University of Washington, 72–73
    University of Washington poll, 96
Project 21 black think tank, 83
Public Broadcasting System, 123

Q

Quinn, Jim, 70–71
Quinn, Justin, 34–37
Quinnipiac University, 80, 95

R

Racial views of the Tea Party
　absence of proof of racism, 80–83, 87–89
　attitudes towards blacks, 72–73
　conservative movement, 75–76
　disgust with Obama, 27, 62–65, 69–70
　eliminationist rhetoric, 85–86
　exposure of bigotries, 72–73
　hyperbolic claims, 84–89
　mainstream attitudes, 72–75
　real racism, 66–68
　subtle racism, 68–70
　"taking government back" rhetoric, 62–63, 77–78
　Tim Scott's election, 56
　See also Tea Party: The Documentary Film
Rallies (Tea Party rallies)
　absence of violence, 85
　Boehner's appearances, 141
　comments by Santelli, 33
　eliminationist rhetoric, 85–86
　Rand Paul appearances, 62
　Ron Paul appearances, 18
　Sarah Palin appearances, 83
Rasmussen, Scott, 58, 119
Reagan, Ronald (the "Gipper")
　conservative views of, 106
　"80 percent rule," 124
　tax rates during presidency, 169
　Tea Party idolization of, 108

Real Clear Politics website, 72
Reason (Libertarian magazine), 84, 113
Reconstruction Era (US), 55
Reform Party (Ross Perot), 52
Reichskristallnacht ("Night of Broken Glass") (Germany), 84
Reid, Harry, 24, 132–133
Republican Governors Association, 100
Republican Party
　absorption of Tea Party, 141–144
　Brown's Massachusetts victory, 23
　defeat by Obama (2008), 19
　immigration reforms beliefs, 118–119
　Jewish Republican congressmen, 122
　Krugman's stance against, 86
　laissez-faire instincts, 119
　myth of small government belief, 112–114
　need for the Tea Party, 142–143
　negative effect of Tea Party on elections, 123–125
　"Pledge to America," 96
　similarities with Tea Party, 95–96
　takeover by Tea Party, 53
　Tea Party foreign policy vs., 117–122
　Tea Party threats, 45–46, 160–161
　traditionalists vs. Tea Party, 25
　transformation of, 148–149
　ultraconservative faction, 103–111

voting similarities of Tea Party, 95
Republicans in name only (RINOs), 150
Restore America's Legacy (RAL), conservative PAC, 29–30
Rich, Frank, 80, 86, 88
Right Wing News, 59
"A Roadmap for America's Future" (Ryan), 165
Robertson, Dale, 67, 68
Robinson, Eugene, 62–65, 77
Roosevelt, Theodore, 52
Rove, Karl, 68
Rubio, Marco
　call for balanced budget amendment, 97
　midterm election victory, 24, 32–33, 94, 97, 130
　Palin's endorsement of, 128
Russo, Sal, 35
Rutgers University, 52
Rutten, Tim, 99–102
Ryan, Paul D., 101, 165

S

Salon.com article, 72
Same-sex marriage, 55, 57, 151, 156–157
San Francisco Chronicle report, 58
Santelli, Rick, 19, 31, 33
Schiavo, Terri, 113
Schoen, Douglas, 119
Scott, Tim, 55–56
Senate
　Banking, House, Urban Affairs Committee, 34
　election of Rand Paul, 24
　election of Ron Paul, 20
　food safety bill passage, 43

midterm (2010) elections, 20, 23–24, 32
Nevada, Kentucky primaries, 29
white (Caucasian) dominance, 66
September 11, 2001 terrorist attack, 69, 88
September 12 March on Washington, 57
Shadow Party (of Soros), 149
Shields, Mark, 123–125
Skoda, Mark A., 143
Small government beliefs, 112–114
Snowe, Olympia, 45, 160
Social Security, 21, 119
Soros, George, 146, 149
South Korea, free trade pact, 119
Steinglass, Matt, 138–140
Stern, Howard, 67
Stossel, John, 113
Stout, Paul, 68, 69–70
Sullivan, Andrew, 138–139

T

"Taking government back" rhetoric, 62–63, 77–78
Tancredo, Tom, 41
TARP (Troubled Asset Relief Program), 3, 19, 63, 68, 169
Tax Day 2008 protests, 78
Tax reform, 105, 108
"The Tea Partiers' Racial Paranoia" (Salon.com), 72
Tea Party: The Documentary Film, 58
Tea Party Caucus (Capitol Hill), 141

The Tea Party Goes to Washington (Rand Paul), 93
Tea Party Movement
  absorption by Republican Party, 141–144
  accusations against, 28
  advantages vs. populist movements, 35–37
  agenda for change, 28–30
  anti-black president sentiment, 62–65
  betrayal of individual members, 136–137
  chaos creation possibility, 163–171
  comparison to Nazi movement, 84–86
  "Contract from America," 96, 105–111
  demographics, 75
  exaggerations of importance of, 43–46
  exploitation from corporate funding, 47–49
  hatred of NAFTA, 134
  health care crisis solution, 109
  immigration reform beliefs, 118–119
  inauthenticity of, 38–42
  midterm election victories, 19–20, 23–24, 31–33
  national convention, 39–40, 47, 115, 127–128
  origins, 18–19, 31–32
  progressive views of, 20–21
  protests (2009), 23
  racism component, 66–71
  reasons for possible failure, 156–159
  representation of mainstream concerns, 26–30
  Republican radical identification, 100–102
  single goal of, 105
  strength in Republican identification, 138–140
  "taking government back" rhetoric, 62–63, 77–78
  ultraconservative views of, 103–111
  voting like Republicans, 95
Tea Party Nation, 53, 127
Tea Party Patriots (umbrella group), 130–131
"Tea Party Plan for Next Phase" (*Wall Street Journal*), 94
TeaParty.org, 67
Temple, William, 48
Texas, illegal alien problems, 35
Third Party political party
  support for, 50–51
  takeover of Republican Party, 53
  Tea Party as, 51–52
  unknowns of, 52–53
Thurmond, Strom, 55
Times/CBS poll, 74
Torture/torture facilities
  conservative policy, 103
  Coulter vs. Rand Paul viewpoints, 115
  institutionalism of, 139
  libertarian opposition, 104
"True North" political principles, 150–151, 153
2010 midterm elections. *See* Midterm elections (2010)

U

Ultraconservative Republicanism, 103–111

United We Stand America (political movement), 139
University of Washington poll, 72–73, 96
US Chamber of Commerce, 43–44, 135–136
Utah primary election, 161

V

Vanity Fair magazine, 88
"Victories Suggest Wider Appeal of Tea Party" (Rand Paul, Marco Rubio), 94
Viguerie, Richard, 120

W

Wall Street bailouts, 134
Wall Street Journal
    op-ed, report, 97–98, 131
    Tea Party manifesto comments, 166
Wallace, George, 60
Walsh, Joan, 72
Washington Post articles, 74–75, 77, 81, 86–87
Watts, J. C., 55
Weigel, Dave, 138
Weiler, Jonathan D., 40
We've Been Had: How Obama and the Radicals Conned Middle Class America (Keena), 145
Whatley, Stuart, 38–41
Whites (Caucasian)
    attitudes towards blacks, 72–73
    dominance in the Senate, 66
    nationalist Tea Party members, 57–61
World Trade Organization (WTO), 134
WorldNetDaily.com (Joseph Farah), 47

Y

Yardley, Jim, 156–159
Yglesias, Matthew, 138
You Have the Power: How to Take Back Our Country and Restore Democracy in America (Dean), 78
Young, Cathy, 72–76

Z

Zernike, Kate, 117–118
Zeskind, Leonard, 60
Zhirinovsky, Vladimir, 139

www.ingramcontent.com/pod-product-compliance
Lightning Source LLC
Chambersburg PA
CBHW071921290426
44110CB00013B/1439